OVERTURE OP

in associati

We are delighted to have the opportunity to work with Overture Publishing on this series of opera guides and to build on the work English National Opera did over twenty years ago on the Calder Opera Guide Series. As well as reworking and updating existing titles, Overture and ENO have commissioned new titles for the series and all of the guides will be published to coincide with repertoire being staged by the company at the London Coliseum.

We hope that these guides will prove an invaluable resource now and for years to come, and that by delving deeper into the history of an opera, the poetry of the libretto and the nuances of the score, readers' understanding and appreciation of the opera and the art form in general will be enhanced.

John Berry
Artistic Director, ENO

The publisher John Calder began the Opera Guides series under the editorship of the late Nicholas John in association with English National Opera in 1980. It ran until 1994 and eventually included forty-eight titles, covering fifty-eight operas. The books in the series were intended to be companions to the works that make up the core of the operatic repertory. They contained articles, illustrations, musical examples and a complete libretto and singing translation of each opera in the series, as well as bibliographies and discographies.

The aim of the present relaunched series is to make available again the guides already published in a redesigned format with new illustrations, updated reference sections and a literal translation of the libretto that will enable the reader to get closer to the meaning of the original. New guides of operas not already covered will be published alongside the redesigned ones from the old series.

Gary Kahn
Series Editor

Sponsors of the Overture Opera Guides

for the 2012/13 Season at ENO

La traviata

Giuseppe Verdi

Overture Opera Guides
Series Editor
Gary Kahn

Editorial Consultant
Philip Reed

OVERTURE

OVERTURE OPERA GUIDES
in association with

Overture Publishing
an imprint of

ALMA CLASSICS
London House
243-253 Lower Mortlake Road
Richmond
Surrey TW9 2LL
United Kingdom

Printed in United Kingdom by TJ International, Padstow, Cornwall

ISBN: 978-1-84749-551-8

Contents

List of Illustrations

1. Giuseppe Verdi in the mid-1850s, soon after the premiere of *La traviata*, photographed by André-Adolphe-Eugène Disdéri.

2. Francesco Maria Piave, the librettist of *La traviata* (above).
3. Alexandre Dumas *fils*, author of the novel and the play
La Dame aux camélias (below).

4. Marie Duplessis, the original model for Violetta Valéry and lover of, among many others, Alexandre Dumas *fils*. She died, two weeks after her twenty-third birthday, in 1847.

5. Engraving of the Teatro La Fenice, Venice, in the early nineteenth century, with opera-goers arriving by gondola. 6. Cover of vocal score published at the time of the first performances in 1853. Note the costumes showing the action taking place in the seventeenth century, as prescribed by the censor.

Early Violettas:
7. Fanny Salvini-Donatelli (top left), who sang at the premiere. 8. Maria Spezia (top right). 9. Marietta Piccolomini (bottom left). 10. Adelina Patti (bottom right).

Violettas of the first half of the twentieth century:
11. Geraldine Farrar (above).
12. Rosa Ponselle (below).

13. Claudia Muzio (above).
14. Licia Albanese (below).

15. Maria Callas in the production directed by Luchino Visconti
and designed by Lila de Nobili at La Scala, Milan, in 1955.

16. Renato Cioni as Alfredo and Mirella Freni as Violetta in the production directed and designed by Franco Zeffirelli at La Scala, Milan, in 1964 (above).
17. Luciano Pavarotti as Alfredo and Renata Scotto as Violetta in the production directed by Tyrone Guthrie and designed by Sophie Fedorovitch at the Royal Opera House in 1965 (below).

18. Patrick Wheatley as Germont and Valerie Masterson as Violetta in the production directed by John Copley and designed by David Walker at ENO in 1979 (above). 19. Plácido Domingo as Alfredo and Cornell MacNeil as Germont in the production directed by Colin Graham and designed by Tanya Moiseiwitsch at the Metropolitan Opera in 1981 (below).

20. Plácido Domingo as Alfredo and Teresa Stratas as Violetta in the 1983 film *La traviata* directed by Franco Zeffirelli (above). 21. Angela Gheorghiu as Violetta and Frank Lopardo as Alfredo in the production directed by Richard Eyre and designed by Bob Crowley at the Royal Opera House in 1994 (below).

22. Julia Roberts and Richard Gere in their opera box to see *La traviata* in the 1990 film *Pretty Woman* (above): see pp. 47–48. 23. Christine Schäfer as Violetta in the production directed by Peter Mussbach and designed by Erich Wonder at the Staatsoper, Berlin in 2003 (below).

24. Patrizia Ciofi as Violetta and Dmitri Hvorostovsky as Germont in the production directed by Robert Carsen and designed by Patrick Kinmonth for the reopening of La Fenice, Venice, in 2004 (above). 25. Anna Netrebko as Violetta in the production directed by Willy Decker and designed by Wolfgang Gussmann at the Salzburg Festival in 2005 (below).

26. Talise Trevigne as Violetta and the giant doll that dominated Act One in the production directed by Graham Vick and designed by Paul Brown at the National Indoor Arena, Birmingham for Birmingham Opera Company in 2007 (above).

27. Federico Lepre as Alfredo and Carmen Giannattasio as Violetta in the production directed by David McVicar and designed by Tanya McCallin at Scottish Opera in 2008 (below).

28. Jonas Kaufmann as Alfredo and Anna Netrebko as Violetta in the
production directed by Richard Eyre and designed by Bob Crowley,
restaged at the Royal Opera House in 2008 (above).
29. Corinne Winters as Violetta in the production directed by Peter
Konwitschny and designed by Johannes Leiacker at ENO in 2013 (below).

An Introduction to *La traviata*

Nicholas John

Verdi's eighteenth opera is based on *La Dame aux camélias*, a play written by Alexandre Dumas *fils*, which Dumas had dramatized from his own best-selling novel published in 1848. Verdi lived from 1847 to 1849 in Paris with the soprano Giuseppina Strepponi, who was eventually to become his second wife. So he knew Parisian society from personal experience and was able to see the play in which it was so controversially portrayed as soon as the censor lifted the ban on its performance in 1852.

Verdi's early operas deal with major biblical and historical subjects. In 1849, however, he composed *Luisa Miller*, based on Schiller's drama *Kabale und Liebe*, a private tragedy that does not involve the public lives of the characters. In the following year, he asked the Venetian stage poet Francesco Maria Piave to turn a modern domestic tragedy into a libretto for him: *Le Pasteur* by Émile Souvestre and Eugène Bourgeois. This opera, which was performed as *Stiffelio* in 1850, concerns a Protestant German pastor's forgiveness of his wife's adultery. The censor demanded drastic alterations to the text for its first performance in Trieste, because there were many quotations from the Bible. As a result, the story and especially the magnificent final scene were badly mutilated. Despite its failure, Verdi's high opinion of the score may be judged from his decision eight years later to rework it as *Aroldo*, in which a similar theme of forgiven adultery is set in the period of the Crusades.

Suggestions for his next opera, commissioned by La Fenice – the main theatre in Venice, where the censorship was more sympathetic than elsewhere – ranged from *Manon Lescaut* to *King Lear*. Although Verdi had not come to any settled conclusion that domestic subjects were alone suitable for his operas, he did want to break out of the restricting traditions of Italian opera – the conventional forms as well as subjects. A composer was expected to write set pieces ('numbers') which should, by convention, be handled in certain ways. The aria, for instance, was to be introduced by a *scena*, or dramatic recitative, and then to contain two movements – a lyrical passage in usually moderate tempo with a fast closing section (the *cabaletta*). But Verdi wrote to Salvatore Cammarano, the librettist of *Il trovatore*, around this time, expressing his dissatisfaction with such restrictions and saying that they should not have to make *Lear* a drama in the traditional form, 'but treat it in an entirely novel manner, on a vast scale, and without regard to conventions of any kind'.[1]

At this turning point in his artistic career, Verdi chose to collaborate with Piave on Victor Hugo's play *Le Roi s'amuse* – banned for decades in France because it showed a reigning (sixteenth-century) monarch to be highly immoral. The score, which he called 'an interminable string of duets',[2] did indeed break many conventions. The characters, apart from the soprano heroine, Gilda, are wholly exceptional by Italian operatic standards. It was, however, a huge success, and the management invited the same team to write another piece for the theatre. In the meantime, a wild and little-known Spanish drama by Antonio García Gutiérrez had caught the composer's imagination to fill a commission for the 1852/53 season in Rome. *Il trovatore* was completed by July 1852 and performed in January 1853. Piave began work on his remarkably skilful distillation of Dumas's play in November 1852, and the music of *La traviata* was hurriedly composed for performances in April. Work on these two operas, so different in subject, thus overlapped. Devices such as the tenor's serenade offstage (*Il trovatore*, Act Four; *La traviata*, Act One), while the soprano holds the stage alone, or the introduction of slow, lyrical

---

1   See David R.B. Kimbell, *Verdi in the Age of Italian Romanticism* (Cambridge: Cambridge University Press, 1981), p. 250.

2   See John Rosselli, *The Life of Verdi* (Cambridge: Cambridge University Press, 2000), p. 98.

passages such as 'Ai nostri monti' or 'Parigi, o cara' in the climactic final scenes, illustrate their kinship. Both operas also contain set numbers which are absolutely traditional in style: 'Tacea la notte' or 'Il balen' in *Il trovatore*, the *Brindisi* or 'Di Provenza il mar' in *La traviata*. Nevertheless, *La traviata* develops to the furthest point so far in Verdi's career the flexible word-setting for dramatic effect that broke through the 'closed forms' of Italian operatic convention. There are few such dramatically successful dialogues as that of Violetta and Alfredo in Act One, or Violetta and Germont in Act Two.

Although Verdi lost his battle to have the opera staged in contemporary dress, its shocking topicality was not lost on audiences, and it was roundly condemned for immorality in many countries. *The Times*, after its UK premiere on 24th May 1856, inveighed against its 'foul and hideous horrors' and no English translations of the libretto were sold. It was, of course, the character of the fallen woman (*la traviata* literally means 'the woman led astray') which attracted Verdi in the first place. In her, as in the character of Rigoletto, vice and virtue are combined; whereas the jester's love for his daughter redeems his utterly vicious qualities, Violetta is a courtesan called upon to be an example of noble self-sacrifice in a venal, materialistic society.

La traviata rapidly came to vie with *Il trovatore* in popularity, despite the very odd mixture of period costumes in which it was performed and the extraordinary alterations demanded by censors and managements in different places. (References to '*croce e delizia*' – literally 'cross and delight' – became 'pain and delight' in some versions; Alfredo became Rodolfo Dermont in Naples in 1855, and Rodolphe d'Orbel in Paris in 1864 – where Dr Grenvil became Dr Germont!) The title page of printed scores up to 1914 set the action around 1700, and Shaw observed in 1890 that every opera-goer was familiar with 'Violetta in the latest Parisian confections and Alfredo in full Louis XIV fig'![3] Verdi, however, never went back to this type of intimate contemporary subject. After 1853 he turned back to history, Schiller and Shakespeare for subjects and a new scale of operatic composition.

---

3   G.B. Shaw, *Shaw's Music: The Complete Musical Criticism of Bernard Shaw* (London: The Bodley Head, 1981), p. 229.

La traviata: From Real Life to Opera

Denis Arnold

Verdi's choice of *La Dame aux camélias* as the subject for an opera was both original and a stroke of genius. There was no other work in which he could have found a model for such an opera. Admittedly, the medium affected the message. We may suspect that the heroine of the original true-life story of Dumas *fils*'s love affair with a courtesan was hardly acceptable as a role for an operatic diva of the 1850s; even in Dumas's novel, in which he first idealizes her, she is – though a woman of charm and grace – a swearing, drinking young woman, who was far from the conventional heroine. Her red camellias worn on the days of the month when she was 'not available' acknowledged a physical fact not generally referred to in polite society. In the play based on his novel and in which Dumas took one further step back from reality, the meaning of these camellias was absent, along with the lewd language – as well as much of the obvious enjoyment of the promiscuity in which the heroine indulges. From the play, it is no great distance to Francesco Maria Piave's libretto for Verdi's opera, and although there are necessary cuts which may damage its delicate psychology, the courtesan now emerges as the victim of self-sacrifice, which fits in well with the conventions of Romantic opera. But this hitherto unknown approach to Realism posed such problems that Verdi never attempted such a subject again, and when the *verismo* composers of the *fin de siècle* followed up his suggestion, they vulgarized his conception.

The difficulties were, in the first place, those of musical language. Realism involves an abandonment of at least the most improbable operatic conventions, the inevitable succession of cavatina and cabaletta and the reliance on aria. Verdi, never a revolutionary, had yet more or less solved these problems in *Rigoletto*, with its single true full-scale aria, 'Caro nome', and its exploitation of a peculiarly subtle accompanied recitative and arioso, the result of the development of techniques known to Rossini and Donizetti which, by using the orchestra to give continuity of melody, allowed the action to continue naturally without the protagonists singing in clear-cut patterns. The strong, regular musical phrases, the constant repetition of tight, short rhythmic motifs, no doubt appropriate to the heroic figures of historical drama, do not fit the bourgeois, unheroic characters of this new style of story. A more conversational melody has to be created for both orchestra and voice. When Verdi said that he considered *Rigoletto* his favourite from a professional point of view, he probably meant that he had succeeded in precisely this; when he declared that as an amateur (a word which implies 'love' rather than technical perfection) he had a preference for *La traviata*, he may well have been referring to his compromise – for there is much of the old cavatina/cabaletta here, though subsumed into the continuous flow of music in such a highly imaginative way that we may agree to disagree with his own assessment: for what greater skill is there than the assimilation of existing, well-tried forms into something new?

Finally, there was a need for a new orchestration. Again, *Rigoletto* had led the way. The composer who used the low register of the clarinet and the high one of a muted double bass to convey the sinister atmosphere of the assassin's alley near the Mincio was ready for further adventures in sound. It was in *La traviata* that these were most successful.

Act One

The Prelude to Act One shows at once a new approach to Italian opera. It is a tone picture in two parts. The opening [1],[1] to be heard again at the beginning of Act Three, when Violetta is dying,

---

1 Numbers in square brackets refer to the Thematic Guide on pp. 69–73. [Ed.].

is surely an expression of the frailty of the heroine. The delicacy of the scoring is particularly beautiful, the violins divided in a way not unlike that in the Prelude to Wagner's *Lohengrin* or the Overture to Weber's *Euryanthe* (neither of which Verdi probably knew at this time), the dynamic markings insisting both on the quietest of tone and (by accents on weak beats of the bar) sustained sound; while the heartbreak is conveyed by the broken motif as the melody rises to the climax. The second phase includes the famous melody associated with Violetta's love for Alfredo (to appear later as [16]). The dynamics again are full of *pianissimi*, with *forte* only at the moments of passion, when the cellos burst twice into the *diminuendo*.

After this, it comes as a shock for the curtain to go up on a party – and on brash party music [2]. The music which would normally be played by a wind band on the stage (as in *Rigoletto*) is now given to the orchestra in the pit; and soon it is plain that this is part of the building up of 'natural' atmosphere, for the voices vie with the music as at real parties, while the tunes change from time to time in the manner of dances at balls. Against this, the characters are introduced to us – and each other: Violetta and her multitudinous guests, who include her 'protector', the Baron Douphol, her friend Flora and the young attractive Alfredo, who is introduced by one Gaston. As yet they are not strongly differentiated, and it is only as they take supper that the situation begins to emerge. The Baron is already jealous of Alfredo, who, Gaston has revealed, called at Violetta's house every day two years ago when she had been ill. When she asks the Baron to lead a toast, he refuses. She passes the invitation over to Alfredo, who accepts.

The following *Brindisi* [3] (or drinking song) is the first real interruption to the dance music; and yet its insertion does not seem to break up the continuity (Verdi has, in any case, finished in the wrong key so as to make the conclusion of the section indecisive). Like the Duke's *Ballata* in *Rigoletto*, which arrives at the same stage in the action, the *Brindisi* is a direct, memorable tune (though Verdi does not want just a brash rendering, being careful to mark the tenor's verse '*con grazia, leggerissimo*', and the decorative 'turn' figure at the end of the first full phase is *pianissimo*). But the chorus can take it up without danger, and the subsequent division of the melody between Violetta and Alfredo is a natural way of showing their increasing affection. The dance music is resumed (there is now a real stage band to play a waltz [4]). Suddenly Violetta feels faint, to the alarm of her guests, most especially Alfredo. The fact that life goes on inexorably is pointed out by the sublime indifference of the band, which continues playing the waltz while the lovers, now alone, have the opportunity to reveal their feelings – a broken, consumptive melody for Violetta and Alfredo's ardent love shown by the gradual building-up of his part into what at first seems to be an aria. 'Un dì felice' ('One blessed day') [5] is memorable for its insistence on a rhythmic fragment:

which is welded into a grand climax that seems vaguely familiar, because it is related to the second section of the Prelude [6]; and for an unexpected turn to the minor key to express the mysterious delights of love.

The aria now turns into a duet [7], as Violetta replies with flirtatious *fioriture* (ornamental turns); her increasing love is expressed in later phrases, in which falling chromatic figures convey deeper feeling. There is a duet cadenza, which is the first real reminder of operatic conventions. Then Gaston returns, and with him the insensitive world suggested by the waltz played by the stage band. Alfredo and Violetta say their farewells, and the guests depart to the opening music of the act, the stage band swallowed up by the brassy full orchestra.

At this moment we realize that there have been events, but no conspicuous break in the music, no recitative, no formal aria – though plenty of good tunes. How it has been done is almost miraculous;

and such is the extended nature of the scene that to call the final stage of the party 'Stretta [a fast concluding section] *dell' Introduzione Atto I*', as someone (Verdi himself?) has done in the score, seems absurd. 'Introduction' indeed! We are now far into the action. Only from the singer's point of view can it be so imagined: for now comes the first true recitative and aria. Violetta is alone and muses over the events of the evening. Her recitative is so well thought out that we (and the conductor) must wonder whether the orchestra's first notes should be a dramatic *tremolando* or a measured, quasi-thematic motif (the notation could mean either). In any case, the aria [9] is masterly. Its first section, 'Ah, fors'è lui' ('Ah, perhaps he is the one'), in the minor key, reveals Violetta's new-found love; and the second phase, 'A quell'amor' ('The love that beats'), is in fact Alfredo's proclamation of his love, 'Di quell'amor' [6], in the major key as it must be, but complete with the mysterious tinge of the minor key – that juxtaposition of '*croce e delizia*' which is the essence of the opera. The second strophe, complete with cadenza, is often omitted in performance. In accompanied recitative, she numbers the reasons for putting aside her fantasy. With a cadenza, she tells herself to enjoy her usual hedonistic life of love, and the following cabaletta, 'Sempre libera degg'io' ('I must be entirely free') [10], would conclude the matter (and the act) in a conventional opera. But Alfredo is heard singing of his love and yet again of 'croce e delizia' under the balcony. Violetta's mood infects this too and her brilliant *fioriture* express her feverish excitement and her frantic determination to enjoy the pleasures of life.

Act Two

Critics have noted that by cutting out the emotional development embodied in the second act of Dumas's play, where the point is made that the lovers cannot afford to live together unless the heroine continues to give herself to her rich protector, Piave and Verdi have made a rather abrupt transition to the already achieved domesticity of their second act. But opera does not need to work in the manner of a well-made play and can assume gaps of several months in the action. Within a few bars of its opening, Act Two seems quite natural in atmosphere. The scene is a bourgeois country house near Paris, and Alfredo enters in bourgeois country clothes. After a few bars of introduction, he tells us in an at first conventional accompanied recitative of his contentment, living with his beloved; the recitative moves into arioso for a moment of passionate expression of his delight that Violetta has also given up her past life for him; and this leads naturally into the aria 'De' miei bollenti spiriti / il giovanile ardore' ('The youthful ardour / of my passionate nature') [11], its urgency of emotion conveyed partly by the strange orchestral accompaniment with repeated notes by bowed cellos and basses and plucked upper strings, partly by the rapid alterations of *fortes* in the tenor's upper register and *pianissimi* phrases.

The atmosphere is broken by a return to the brittle quaver figure which has been heard in the brief introduction to the act. The maid Annina comes in breathless and, in answer to Alfredo's question, replies that she has been to Paris to sell her mistress's horses and carriages to pay for the expensive luxury of an idyllic country life. To the brittle quavers is now added a rhythm more often associated with funeral marches, as Alfredo realizes the disastrous situation and his hitherto extraordinary lack of perception; the march-like rhythm and quaver figure turn into the expression of his determination to ride to Paris to remedy the situation. His next set piece 'O mio rimorso' ('Oh, what remorse') is really the cabaletta to 'De' miei bollenti spiriti', though it has been inserted into the action so cleverly that we hardly notice that, and it comes the nearest to the grand manner of *Il trovatore* that is to be found in the opera, with insistent vocal motifs and military rhythms in the orchestra. When he has left, Violetta enters with Annina, who explains that Alfredo has gone to Paris. There is now the first piece of extended recitative in the opera, as Violetta first reads a letter from Flora inviting her to a ball (this, as we shall see, preparing the way for the next scene), an invitation Violetta is not disposed to accept. Then her manservant ushers in a man who introduces himself as Alfredo's father, Giorgio Germont. Germont accuses Violetta of ruining his son, who has expressed the intention of selling his possessions. The truth is very different, Violetta says, giving Germont a paper proving that it is *she* who is selling *her* property. Germont is taken aback (the orchestra underlines this with a curious short repeated phrase), but suggests that it is her guilty past that is making her do this. In a great outburst she says that it is her love for Alfredo that governs her life now. Germont realizes that he must appeal to her to make a noble sacrifice. Even before he asks her to leave his son, she feels the impending disaster, as the orchestral *tremolando* makes clear. His plea opens the duet 'Pura siccome un angelo / Iddio mi die' una figlia' ('God granted me a daughter / who is as pure as an angel') [12], in which he tells her that she is ruining the chances of marriage for Alfredo's sister. Violetta's anguished reply is given first in a kind of broken recitative, as the orchestra develops an agitated figure; and the passionate ebb and flow of the argument between them is expressed by rapid changes of tonality, culminating in Violetta's statement of the depth of her love for Alfredo, which clearly Germont cannot understand. The shortness of phrase and repetitiveness of the melody [13] lead into a truly expansive section 'Ah, il supplizio è sì spietato' ('Ah, it would be so cruel a torment'):

which takes Germont aback. He admits that giving up Alfredo will be a great sacrifice for her – but then pursues his case. She is now young and beautiful, but in the way of things, Alfredo is unlikely to remain in love with her as she grows older – and then what will happen? The nagging insistence of yet another short motif wears her down and eventually she gives in. She tells Germont in a most memorable lyrical passage, 'Dite alla giovine' ('Tell your daughter') [14], that he can tell his daughter that she will sacrifice herself; and Germont is moved and comforts her in a melody which frequently clashes against the harmonies, Verdi miraculously drawing the two themes together as the pair grieve in their different ways. The climactic cadenza finished, they have to take practical steps. In recitative Germont tells her that she must tell Alfredo she does not love him – but she knows that Alfredo will just not believe her. If she leaves him he will follow. To give her courage, she asks Germont to embrace her, and then she sits down to write a note to her beloved. From arioso, the music moves into another quasi-march rhythm as she thinks she will die, Germont trying to comfort her with the thought that she will soon forget and resume her happiness. Before Germont leaves, they again embrace, indicating the true emotional bond which has grown between them. The musical motif of the word '*sacrifizio*' ('sacrifice') underlines Violetta's mood, and after Germont has gone the rhythm provides a link into the next stage of the action. She rings for Annina to take a note to an address which surprises the maid (though we are not told it) – and the strangeness of Violetta's mood is hinted at in a hesitant, anguished melody for the clarinet. Violetta is thrown into confusion by Alfredo's return (the orchestral accompaniment tells us of her agitation). Alfredo is clearly baffled by the change in atmosphere and a nervously inconsequential conversation follows, in which the music never seems to develop properly. Suddenly Violetta cries out 'Amami, Alfredo' ('Love me, Alfredo'). The melody, which is related to her expression of love in their Act One duet, 'Di quell'amor' [6], now appears in the form we first heard it in the Prelude. '*Con passione e forza*' is the instruction – but it is brief, and with a quick 'goodbye' (significantly turning to the minor key for just a single note) she runs out into the garden.

Alfredo, not surprisingly, is now completely baffled – but not particularly disturbed, although the orchestra conveys a sense of unease. A servant enters with Violetta's letter. Alfredo has only to read the opening to realize she has left him and jumps to the assumption that she has returned to the luxuries provided by her old protector. His anguish is as sudden as Violetta's had been a few minutes ago (the change of key and the use of the orchestral tutti are both very similar), but his father, having entered from the garden, tries to comfort him, attempting to bring him to his senses by reminding him of his family home in Provence, in an expressive aria [17]. This is very consistent in tone with his patriarchal address to Violetta earlier (and if the calm, much-to-be-respected father figures seem the stuff of nineteenth-century Italian opera, it may be said that they are still by no means uncommon in latter-day middle-class Italian society). Alfredo is not really convinced; the unease returns both between the strophes of the aria and at its end. He catches sight of Flora's invitation, guesses where to find Violetta and dashes off, followed by his father, to confront her.

The scene changes to Flora's mansion, the mood of the party music of Act One returns (the dance music [18] again in the pit rather than given to the stage band) and, as before, a conversation between the characters is given musical continuity in the orchestra. A ballet of fancy-dressed guests (as is suitable for a work with a French subject, since a ballet was a *sine qua non* at the Paris Opéra) begins with a group of gypsies [19]. During this, Flora engages in gossip with friends. Will Violetta come (presumably with the Baron, who seems now again to be in favour) or will Alfredo, who has also been invited? The ballet resumes with Spanish bullfighters [20], much applauded by the other guests, including Flora's immediate friends. The gaiety is interrupted by the entrance of Alfredo, who is followed shortly by Violetta, on the arm of the Baron. The minor key, a shifty theme [21] played by violins and clarinets in an uncomfortable lower register, conveys the immediate unease. Violetta is taken aback on seeing Alfredo, and her anguish is clear from her phrase 'Ah, perché venni, incauta' ('Ah, why was I so rash as to come') [22], the lyricism of which is strangely at odds with the tense, febrile music of the others. Alfredo insists on playing at cards for high stakes with his rival (as it seems to him), the Baron. Alfredo cleans him out, the atmosphere electric as the Baron needles him with the saying 'Sfortuna nell'amore / fortuna reca al giuoco' ('Unlucky in love, / lucky at cards '). The tension is broken when they go off to supper. There is an uneasy cadence before Violetta returns, followed by Alfredo. She tells him to leave at once. Alfredo believes that she thinks it might come to a duel in which the Baron could be killed, but, in heroic tone expressed in another finely rhythmic melody, he sings that he does not care whether he, Alfredo, will die, because he will have had his revenge. Violetta protests that it is not the Baron for whom she is afraid, but him. He begs her to leave with him, but she refuses. To a significant and terrifying orchestral tutti he flings open the door of the anteroom and calls the others to hear. His accusation is made in yet another melody built from short repetitive rhythmic motifs: this woman spent her fortune on me – now I pay her back. He flings his winnings on the floor. There is a moment of pandemonium while everybody sings *'velocissimo'* [23]. Then his father, who has arrived unannounced, takes control. He is ashamed of his son (though since he alone knows the whole story, this patriarchal gesture is surely more than a little unjust) and is prepared to disown him. Alfredo, in a nervous motif, is shocked; Violetta, *'con voce debolissima e con passione'*, despairingly says that he understands nothing of her love [25]: and from these different emotions one of the greatest ensembles in Italian opera is built up, as usual in Verdi, with a great melody:

surrounded by significant subsidiary figures; and Verdi, with insight and tact, dispenses with any stretta or vulgar working-up to an artificial fast climax.

Act Three

The extraordinary and beautiful Prelude to this act begins with the music which had begun the whole opera and is similarly scored; but after a few bars the theme is differently developed, for there is now no place for the lively, passionate love theme associated with Alfredo. All is impending death, as is revealed when the curtain rises on Violetta's bedroom. She is deeply sick and attended only by Annina. The themes of the Act's Prelude are used as the background to the conversation of the mistress, the maid and the doctor, who tries to cheer up Violetta with comforting words about convalescence. On the way out he reveals to Annina the truth: there is little time left. Nor does there remain much money. Violetta's only comfort is the letter sent her by Giorgio Germont which she reads aloud, solo strings playing Alfredo's 'Di quell'amor' [6], as she remembers that very first meeting. The emphasis is now surely on the first word of '*croce e delizia*' – the music breaks off suddenly. In a sepulchral voice (the instruction is Verdi's), she speaks: 'È tardi' ('It's getting late') for Alfredo's return promised in Germont's letter. She tries to get up, she looks at her withered body in the mirror and realizes that death is near. She now sings her farewell to life, 'Addio del passato bei sogni ridenti' ('Farewell to those happy dreams of bygone days') [26], a remarkable aria based, as so often in Verdi, on a short motif which recurs in about every bar; and the cruellest part of her fate is that Alfredo, her love for whom is expressed in a single expansive phrase, is not here to comfort her – the oboe's echoes of her obsessive little motif convey the essence of loneliness. Then, as is supposed to happen with consumptives, she suddenly finds her strength again and begs for divine pardon on a penitent sinner. This short passage in the major key gains its musical strength from the orchestral scoring, thick at both bottom and top, the yawning gap in the middle somehow embodying the emptiness of Violetta's life:

But it is too late – the motif of the first section returns and she finishes each strophe (there are two, and to cut the second, as is sometimes done, in my opinion, ruins the proportions of the act) on a top-A *a fil di voce* – no doubt impossible for consumptives, yet extraordinarily moving.

Carnival revellers are heard outside [27], to underline that, as ever, people may be dying, but life goes on. Then, in one of the very few musically weak passages in the whole opera, Annina comes in excitedly to tell Violetta that Alfredo has arrived: the obvious 'link' passage is forgiven when he comes in and, with an enormous outburst, Violetta throws her arms around him. Their excitement is expressed by commonplace but effective broken chords in the orchestra. For a moment hope returns and Alfredo proposes that they should leave Paris and live together: 'Parigi, o cara, noi lasceremo' ('My love, we shall leave Paris') [28]. Violetta sings the second strophe and then they join together – but the fragility of their future prospects is underlined by a curious chromatic figure [28a] which keeps recurring – 'De' corsi affani compenso avrai' ('You will find your reward for what you have suffered') – and is developed into the final cadenza. Realism returns, and in another weak musical link Violetta suddenly becomes pale and Alfredo sends Annina to fetch the doctor. There is a thunderous chord on the brass and Violetta realizes that if Alfredo's return cannot revive her, she is indeed doomed. The lovers sing another duet of a quite different kind – 'Ah! Gran Dio! Morir si giovine' ('Ah! Dear God, to die so young') [29] – the effect of which is gained largely by the way that the *forte* opening rapidly dies away to *pianissimo* and that loud and soft bars are frequently juxtaposed. There is one more climax as Violetta has a further consumptive burst of energy. Then all is lost. Germont arrives, though his words of comfort that he now considers her as his daughter hardly seem enough. The funereal chords which often convey a sense of doom in Verdi (as in the 'Miserere' scene of *Il trovatore*) usher in the end of the opera, as all the characters are now present. Violetta's heroic nature (as opposed to what could have been made into one of pathos – as with Puccini's similar consumptive in *La bohème*) is made still clearer by her hope that Alfredo will find a suitable bride [30]. Hers is a positive, not just a passive love. She suddenly revives, to a wild version of 'Di quell'amor', even ending on a top B flat; then she falls back dead, leaving the others to grieve.

Verdi and *La traviata*:
Two Routes to Realism

Roger Parker

Verdi's *La traviata*, first performed in Venice in 1853, is sometimes called a 'Realist' opera. To many people, this might at first seem a contradiction in terms. How can a form of drama in which people sing (on occasions sing with extreme elaboration) rather than speak, in which their actions are surrounded by opulent orchestral sound, ever be called realist? Perhaps it's better to narrow the terms to something more manageable. Is there anything in the opera's musical workings that might productively be related to the incipient school of Realism then emerging in other arts (the theatre, the novel, the visual arts) in Europe? Even when thus defined, such a question poses severe problems. The very nature of Realism has remained famously problematic even in studies of mid-nineteenth-century literature and the visual arts, in spite of the fact that in those areas it has a clear history – and was used at the time as a banner under which to mark artistic progress. For example, the art historian Linda Nochlin starts her classic survey of the movement by identifying 'a basic cause of confusion bedevilling the notion of Realism', and goes on to explain that the principal difficulty is in the movement's 'ambiguous relationship to the highly problematic concept of reality'.[1] In music history, as the German musicologist Carl Dahlhaus pointed out, these problems are merely compounded: the historical existence of the term in musical genres is tenuous and always fleeting, its usefulness by no means clear. As Dahlhaus writes, this is in part because of frequent

---

1   Linda Nochlin, *Realism* (London: Thames & Hudson, 1971), p. 13.

attempts in the past century to deny that music can *ever* be realistic (a denial related to lingering ideas about 'absolute music'); and in part because of musical historians' continued – and, these days, frankly lazy – insistence on labelling the entire nineteenth century as a period of 'Romanticism', usually thought of as Realism's precursor.[2]

Nevertheless, the challenge of relating these matters to *La traviata* might still be interesting, not least because of the literary text on which it is based. It seems likely that Verdi had seen Alexandre Dumas *fils*'s play *La Dame aux camélias* in Paris soon after it was first performed at the Théâtre du Vaudeville on 2nd February 1852. There is also evidence that his librettist, Francesco Maria Piave, was independently interested in the topic, but it nevertheless seems clear that the composer was immediately struck by the novelty of the play and its operatic possibilities. This is significant, above all, because Dumas's drama, itself based on his novel of the same name published four years earlier, was immediately labelled as an early example of Realism, and was regarded at the time of its creation as a milestone in French drama. Sometimes the play has been linked to Victor Hugo's *Hernani* (1830), which is said to have launched French Romantic drama twenty years earlier. Admittedly, a simple progression from Romanticism (*Hernani*) to Realism (*La Dame aux camélias*) is too simple an account of this heady time of cultural change. The novelty of Dumas's play was not so much as an alternative to the French Romanticism represented by Hugo (a type of drama that was, by and large, dead in the water by 1850), but rather to a new vogue for *comédie vaudeville* and *drame vaudeville* made famous by the dramatist and librettist Eugène Scribe. Dumas largely ignored Scribean precepts, in particular the latter's indispensable, unexpected but carefully prepared denouement, in which morality would triumph. But what struck everyone even more forcibly in *La Dame aux camélias* was Dumas's choice of daring contemporary subject matter, in particular his sympathetic treatment of a prostitute: this was immediately seen as *le réalisme* by critics, and compared to similar efforts in prose and the visual arts.

---

2 See Carl Dahlhaus, *Realism in Nineteenth-century Music*, trans. Mary Whittall (Cambridge: Cambridge University Press, 1985), pp. 1–11.

There is good evidence, then, for thinking that Verdi, ever attracted to novelty in his operatic subject matter, was attracted to elements in the play that were dubbed Realist. However, and to repeat my opening question: how sensible is it to think that his *music* could participate in this kind of artistic renovation? After all, during the 1850s, Verdi's encounter with Dumas appeared almost side by side with a setting of Hugo's arch-Romantic *Le Roi s'amuse* (as *Rigoletto*, 1851) and also frankly Scribean dramas such as *Les Vêpres siciliennes* (1855) and *Un ballo in maschera* (1859). While it is obvious that all these operas have individual characteristics that might be traced to their literary sources, the level of musical difference between them is not remotely comparable to the literary differences between their sources. In other words, those who argue that a Realist Verdi automatically emerged from his encounter with Dumas's play will always be on risky ground; the formal similarities between all Verdi's operas of this period – their shared reliance on old Rossinian numbers such as the multi-movement aria and duet is an obvious case in point – would seem a formidable obstacle. More than this, though, those who posit a Realist Verdi must also deal with the more basic issue mentioned earlier: the issue of whether opera can *ever* be Realist, in the senses (albeit very diverse senses) in which that term is applied to literature or to art.

There are of course many possible routes one might take in going further into this issue: but two in particular appeal to me – two ways in which Verdi's opera might be related to the Realist cause. In following them, we might – I hope – discover something of what makes *La traviata* such an unusual work, even within Verdi's ever-innovative roster of operas during this period.

The first route involves musical characterization, and in particular whether *La traviata*'s somewhat peculiar attitude to its main characters might be a significant step forward in a strain of operatic realism. In early Verdi, not to mention the operas of his Italian predecessors, characters tend to sing in a similar manner, all of them typically indulging in an undifferentiated stream of *bel canto*. But in Verdi operas around *La traviata*, and in that opera in particular, there begins to emerge something that we might call, I hope not too modishly, 'gendered discourse'. To put that matter bluntly, women and men – long deliciously merged and melded on the operatic stage – begin to express themselves differently. This immediately begs a further question: do there emerge musical codes that can be cracked, ones that can reveal the sexual attitudes of the composer and his contemporaries? *La traviata*'s source play, after all, was set in the present day, and Verdi tried to insist on retaining this, even though in the end he was overruled by the Venetian censors. What is more, its plot confronts head-on some of the period's most vexed issues surrounding sexuality; issues that preoccupied people of the time when it was written, but that had rarely or perhaps never before been addressed on the operatic stage. Although the opera was, at its premiere and on subsequent occasions, toned down by the censorship that policed any 'daring' work first produced in Italy, *La traviata* nevertheless retained as its unambiguous backdrop the themes of prostitution and disease. What is more, it addressed the complex relationship between them, the slippery slope that so often led from causal connection to metaphor to divine judgement: from prostitution *and* disease; to prostitution *as* disease; to prostitution *is* disease.

Where Verdi the musician stood on these matters, on the business of what might broadly be called 'cultural morality', is by no means easy to fathom. There are hints, especially in his correspondence with his faithful librettist Francesco Maria Piave, that he occasionally used the services of prostitutes, notably someone called 'Sior Toni' in Venice. There is also the fact that his partner, the soprano Giuseppina Strepponi, had had three illegitimate children during her brief career as an opera singer, and so certainly knew what it was like to stand on the wrong side of a perceived moral divide. With this background in mind, simple connections between biography, music and cultural attitudes can thus be made (and, in the case of *La traviata*, have been made very often). One point seems certain. In Alexandre Dumas *fils*'s novel, *La Dame aux camélias* (1848), which was the basis of his play, the author's fear of and horror at women's bodies are all too evident. The multiple narrative frames within which Dumas enclosed his tale (that 'story within a story' technique so beloved of nineteenth-century novelists) ensure that his heroine has little voice of her own, encased as she is within implacably male perspectives. Indeed, she may be most real and human during the shocking 'flash-forward' near the novel's opening, in which her decaying body is exhumed and displayed to the horrified but fascinated gaze of her former lover. There is of course no trace of this scene in the opera (it would have been unrepresentable on the stage). But what is more important is that in Verdi's version of Dumas's story, Violetta has of course a very real vocal presence. More than this, she is almost throughout the centre of attention. Indeed, it is quite obvious that Verdi was much more interested in her character than in those of the rather wooden and one-dimensional male principals who surround her and compete for her attention. This much is evident from the very first notes of the Prelude to Act One [1], in which her dying gasps are so vividly represented.

Even when agreeing that Violetta's pre-eminence is the general state of affairs, some recent commentators have nevertheless attempted to argue that the heroine suffers from a degree of what we might call musical misogyny. Listen to the first act, they will tell us. Violetta may be prominent, but it is significant that she lacks musical agency, even musical independence. The famous *Brindisi* [3], in which Alfredo toasts the assembled company, is emphatically his song – Violetta merely repeats it after him. And later, in the Act One love duet, Alfredo again is granted what we might call the power of musical invention – he invents the duet's main theme [5] and then looks on admiringly as Violetta weaves a shower of 'feminine' ornaments around it [7]. Even in Violetta's final, act-closing cabaletta, 'Sempre libera degg'io' ('I must be entirely free') [10], in which she obviously dominates the stage, Alfredo's voice again intrudes, insistently reminding us of his musical presence. The same argument might be made in Act Three, in particular about Violetta's grand aria 'Addio del passato bei sogni ridenti' ('Farewell to those happy dreams of bygone days') [26], which goes as far as any aria can in denying 'voice' to the heroine by the realistic touch of making her vocal line painfully fragmentary, continually supplemented by a solo woodwind instrument as she gasps for breath.

Such arguments are in many ways compelling, and certainly offer a powerful way of understanding the opera within the broader cultural context of its time and place. On the other hand, though, there is surely a hint of special pleading about them: a sense that they present an over-literal treatment, a *domestication* of the musical object. For example, it is at least plausible to propose a completely opposite reading of the passages mentioned above. The *Brindisi* may be sung first by Alfredo, but its tendency to delicate ornament makes it more suited to Violetta's vocal capabilities: her verse almost invariably sounds more convincing than his. Similarly, in the love duet the tenor hero may lead off the melodies, but Violetta manages to make them alive by decorating them and altering them to suit her character. And at the end of Act One, Alfredo's most famous melody, 'Di quell'amor' ('A love that beats') [6], is heard only in the distance, while Violetta's reactions to it are much more immediate and impressive. And so the argument could go on, each negative interpretation carrying with it a positive twin.

We clearly need something better than these blunt instruments if we are to go further. Something new might emerge by looking closer at the very centre of the opera, at what most agree is the key vocal and emotional confrontation of the drama: the long duet between Violetta and Germont *père*. In terms of the plot, this is the crucial scene in which Violetta is crushed by patriarchal authority; the voice of patriarchy commands her to sacrifice her feelings on the altar of conventional morality; she acquiesces, only to be rewarded by flamboyantly cruel insults from her lover (Act Two, Scene 2) and an agonizing death (Act Three). Told in these terms the opera fully upholds mid-nineteenth-century attitudes to female sexuality and female freedom: even worse, one could say that it *celebrates* such attitudes.

But all this is primarily a matter of the plot and the words. What does Verdi's music have to do with it? At the start of the Violetta-Germont duet, there emerges a very simple way in which the music might seem indeed to support the play's stern gender stereotypes. The duet is in many ways an emotional dialogue, made up of contrasting sections dominated by each character in turn. And the contrast in musical terms is absolutely clear. Think of Germont's opening melody, 'Pura siccome un angelo / Iddio mi die' una figlia' ('God granted me a daughter / who is as pure as an angel') [12], in which he describes the immaculate purity of his daughter back at home. It presents the very heart of stability and self-assurance: the voice of the patriarch made musical. The regular tread of the accompaniment, the resolute predictability of the phrase structure, the standard manner in which the wind instruments support the voice to round off each phrase, perhaps especially the insistent manner in which the melody returns to one single pitch: all these features gesture in one direction, painting a picture of stability, rationality and, above all, conventionality. Compare this with Violetta's answer 'Non sapete quale affetto / vivo, immense m'arda in petto' ('Don't you realize what a vital, / immense love burns in my heart') [13]. Here we are assailed by a succession of brief, hurried vocal phrases, full of 'sighing' figures that draw attention to the body that utters them, of unpredictable leaps and dynamic shifts, all underpinned by a hesitant, off-beat accompaniment. The extreme musical contrast between Germont's and Violetta's opening statements seems, in other words, to be little more than a musical illustration of the play's governing binary view of gender relations: what is stable and rational is male; what is unstable and emotional is female.

This musical contrast continues through the first part of the duet, as Germont gradually wears down Violetta's resistance. In many ways it is a brutal, uncompromising conflict. But at the very moment of Violetta's capitulation, when she agrees finally to Germont's demand that she renounce Alfredo, something musically extraordinary occurs. This is Violetta's 'Dite alla giovine' ('Tell your daughter') [14], in which she agrees to leave Alfredo and asks Germont to tell his daughter of her sacrifice. In terms of the plot, this juncture might seem to offer merely an intensification of the previous uneven contest. But there is a striking reversal of musical roles. Now it is Violetta who (although her line is marked '*piangendo*' in the score) has the stable, predictable line, the reassuring accompaniment, even the predictable woodwind colour to complete the line. To be sure, her line develops over a long arch through several phrases, having far more directional force than was granted Germont – but that trait merely makes her utterance that much more powerful. By contrast, Germont's answer, 'Piangi, piangi' ('Weep, weep'), is in short, intense phrases that graphically mimic the bodily gesture of weeping. His words here may say that he is magnanimously allowing *her* to cry, 'Piangi, o misera' ('Weep, poor girl'), but the music tells us that it is *he* who is moved to 'feminine' tears, while Violetta has taken control of herself and her destiny.

What are we to conclude from this example? Of course, we could craft yet another interpretation, delving back into the plot to find another way in which Violetta's musical gestures might be seen as merely a further stage in her degradation. But the power of this musical role-reversal, and the compelling force of the heroine's long melody, are surely not so easily dismissed. The masterly placing and serene beauty of 'Dite alla giovine' makes this melody a still point of calm in this scene, indeed in this opera; and from within this still point sings Violetta, solemnly addressing an unknown woman who she hopes will experience none of the trials she herself has undergone. If we accept 'Dite alla giovine' as the crux of the opera, the moment around which the entire action turns, then we might also feel that one-dimensional attitudes to the messages about gender that *La traviata* delivers will always be unsatisfactory. Verdi's realization tells us that, in his elaborately sonorous fictional world, all fixed relationships of musical power are fragile.

My second route to Realism is rather different from the first, although there are connections. It might usefully begin with an important letter by Verdi devoted to the subject. It was written to his publisher Giulio Ricordi and dates from the early 1880s, some thirty years after *La traviata*:

I don't fear cabalettas so much!! And if tomorrow there were born a young man who knew how to do something like, for example, [Bellini's] 'Meco tu vieni o misera' or 'Ah perché non posso odiarti', I would go and hear it with all my heart, and would renounce all the harmonic trifles, all the affectations of our learned orchestration.

Ah, progress, science, realism [...]! Ahi, ahi! Be as realist as you want, but [...] Shakespeare was a realist, but he didn't know it. He was a realist by inspiration; we are realists because of a programme, we are calculated realists. Well then, so be it: system for system, the cabalettas are still better.[3]

This Verdian jeremiad, setting some classic Bellini melodies against the perils of modern opera *circa* 1880 (we can assume he meant those of younger Italian and French composers in particular), is of course one of very many. Closely related is the famous dictum: 'To copy the truth can be a good thing, but *to invent the truth* is better, much better', which also brings Shakespeare (for Verdi the ultimate representative of a 'timeless' artist) to the barricades.[4]

The *terms* in which Verdi talked of Realism in this letter are significant, in that his discussion of 'realist tendencies' seems to hinge on formal matters. Fixed forms such as cabalettas were, by the 1880s, commonly regarded as 'unrealistic', the notion of Realism thus becoming enmeshed with the far broader notion of 'modernity'. There are several problems with this critical move, which has often been repeated in the operatic literature since Verdi. One is that it broadens the notion of Realism to such an extent that it becomes unwieldy as a critical term; another is that it sets up an untenable binary between 'dramatic truth' on the one hand and 'formal fixity' on the other. As hinted earlier, in the case of *La traviata* such a binary is going to be very difficult to sustain. Within the larger picture of Verdi's experiments with formal flexibility during this period it would be hard to single out *La traviata* as a crucial moment, still less one in which the nascent Realism of his literary source had much influence.

One early commentator who was close to Verdi took an interestingly different view on what 'Realism' might mean in technical musical terms. This is the French critic Camille Bellaigue (1858–1930), long associated with the *Revue des deux mondes*, who was a friend

---

3 Letter to Giulio Ricordi concerning the revisions to *Simon Boccanegra*, dated 20th November 1880, in Gaetano Cesari and Alessandro Luzio (eds.), *I copialettere di Giuseppe Verdi* (Milan: Stucchi-Ceretti, 1913), p. 559.

4 Letter to Carla Maffei dated 20 October 1876, *I copialettere*, p. 626.

of both Verdi and Boito, and whose book on the composer, published in 1911, deserves more attention than it gets. Bellaigue, a passionate supporter of the Italian school generally in the polemics then surrounding Wagner, states straight out that, in his opinion, certain radical aspects of Dumas's *La Dame aux camélias* were transferred directly into the music. However, the domain in which he located this transfer had little to do with form:

> No less than I do the poetry, I love the truth, even the 'realism' of *La traviata*. [...] The character and even the condition of the heroine, her entourage, her society – or her dubious society, her demi-monde – in the midst of which she acts and amuses herself: all this is evident right from the start.[5]

To illustrate his point, Bellaigue offers examples that are by our standards vague and impressionistic, if occasionally imbued with extraordinary poetic force. Basically, though, his proposition is not only that *La traviata*'s peculiar ambience is illustrated in the music (a point, after all, made by many, and hardly unique to that opera), but – and crucially – that this ambience is absorbed by the protagonist, making her in a sense at one with her background.

I wonder whether this idea, only touched on by Bellaigue, might be worth pursuing, might even have some broader significance. A brief example might come from two musical numbers that we have already talked about, both critical to the formation of Violetta's musical personality. There's a sense in which her Act One aria 'Ah, fors'è lui' ('Ah, perhaps he is the one') [9] is powerfully related to her aria in Act Three, 'Addio del passato bei sogni ridenti' ('Farewell to those happy dreams of bygone days') [26]. The relationship is both melodic and rhythmic. In the latter case, it resides in the accompaniments, both of which are strongly reminiscent of the obsessive, urban dance rhythms (overwhelmingly that of the waltz) that are so fundamental to the ambience of the opera elsewhere (particularly in its party scene). But there is also, in both cases, an extraordinary simplicity (or, perhaps better, obsession) of melodic

---

5   Camille Bellaigue, *Verdi* (Paris: Laurens, 1911), p. 46.

profile: both arias move insistently around a fixed succession of pitches.

The meaning of this melodic trait can of course be a matter of debate; but the suggestion that it owes much to other moments in the opera is certainly one of the more powerful. Perhaps its closest relative is in fact that very symbol of urban excess, the Act One *Brindisi*. Again we have the driving rhythms, the obsessive return to the same note preceded by rising sixths, the characteristic rhythmic turn figure. It may indeed be significant that the *Brindisi*, 'Ah, fors'è lui' and 'Addio, del passato' were all among Verdi's very earliest musical inspirations for the opera. The last of these is the most poignant. It is as if Violetta's powers of expression are again governed by that urban ambience (she has, after all, returned to Paris); but that now she is trapped by it, the weakening of her body through disease means that she is caught in an infernal machine, the repetitions and obsessive rhythms no longer that of the dance but of time inexorably leaking away.

I have no space here in which to develop further, detailed illustrations, although many could be provided: the manner in which Violetta is, as it were, musically projected through the Parisian ambience is indeed remarkable, and is quite unlike anything found within the other main characters, of this or indeed any other operas in the period. Another obvious example would be the almost obsessive trills that become a prime symbol both of the salon and of Violetta's obsessive gaiety and/ or deceiving surface (one of Verdi's earliest commentators, Abramo Basevi, had a wonderful term for them: '*appoggiature trillate*').[6] We could, I think, be on the edge of something significant here: of finding a way in which an undoubted peculiarity in *La traviata*, the manner in which the heroine is musically related to her ambience, that might be cautiously connected to the business of Realism.

I have sketched two possible routes towards a 'Realist' *La traviata* only in the briefest of detail, but let me nevertheless try to develop some of the reasons why it might have broader significance. One, as some will doubtless have guessed, is that such a conception can have interesting

---

6   Abramo Basevi, *Studio sulle opere di Giuseppe Verdi* (Florence: Tofani, 1859; repr. Bologna: Forni, 1978), p. 235.

resonances with other, interdisciplinary forays into Realism in the arts. Art historians sometimes argue that the Realist movement in the nineteenth century (particularly that associated with Courbet in France) defined itself in part through a distrust of grand rhetorical gestures. Such a formulation might at first seem odd when applied to Verdi: after all, the rhetorical gesture would seem the one true constant of *all* opera. However, if we consider the standard rhetoric of the solo aria, then we might indeed see that Verdi's primary means of character delineation in Violetta's case are significantly different from those in many others, particularly from the hackneyed gestures of her male counterparts in the opera. In a similar manner, we might see connections with the manner – in both Realist literature and art – in which characters tend to grow directly out of their ambience. Hence Flaubert's *Madame Bovary*, with its 'little woman' whose personality is unimaginable without her petty-bourgeois surroundings; hence Courbet's *A Burial at Ornans*, in which the crowd of mourners seem barely to emerge from the earthy background.

More than this, I think the idea of exploring characterization-through-ambience as a trend in later Verdi, and in certain other composers, might also have possibilities. One could, for example, posit a range of Verdian characters in the same 'Realist' line, and this whether or not the ambience from which they emerge is contemporary. Riccardo in *Un ballo in maschera* is probably the classic example, and most would want to add Aida: both seem to project powerful expressions of their opera's dominant colours, and both have character profiles that sharply diverge from that of their co-principals. But the most startling continuation of the trend probably resides in Puccini, most of whose main characters seem at one with their dramatic surrounding. Think of *La bohème*; think of *Tosca*. And lastly there's an obvious (and perhaps comforting) connection to the one opera which everyone agrees *has* to be classed as Realist, and which was so influential for this movement both in France and Italy in the later nineteenth century. I refer of course to Bizet's *Carmen*, with its protagonist who, more than any other, is at one with the ambience – indeed, who creates that ambience virtually single-handed.

As is by now obvious, the ghosts of so many failed attempts to talk sensibly about Realism in music are present around every corner. One thing, though, is certain: in this topic, as in many others musico-logical, some deflation of terms is a good way forward. The idea of Realism in Italian opera, indeed in any opera, will continue to resist strict definition; those formidable obstacles, not least our continuing ambivalence about locating 'pure' musical meaning, will make sure of that. But a better understanding of the entire phenomenon may come if we see more clearly where and how it began. For that reason alone, a journey back to the early 1850s, and to Verdi's *La traviata*, may be useful.

Conspicuous Consumption:
Violetta as Symptom and Subversive

Anna Picard

The cloud of *divisi* strings that opens *La traviata* creates a surface onto which we project our understanding of what is to come. What is it that we hear in those shimmering chords? A faint thread of breath, the gloss of sweat on the forehead of a dying girl, dust motes in the weary air of a sickroom. Violetta is not dead yet. In a moment we will see her dancing, drinking, flirting, living fast, faster, fastest – a fallen woman who falls in love for our pleasure. Along with the fore-warning of death in the first bars, there is a sense of illumination and transfiguration. What Josef von Sternberg did to Marlene Dietrich in the 1932 movie *Shanghai Express* – lighting her from above and transforming that blond, bony brow into something other-worldly and immortal – Verdi did to the consumptive courtesan once known as Rose Alphonsine Plessis.

Giuseppe Verdi and his librettist Francesco Maria Piave were never required to tell Rose Alphonsine's story in *La traviata*. Her progress from *blanchisseuse* to *grande horizontale*, her upwardly-mobile name-change (to Marie Duplessis) and her sordid early death at the age of twenty-three in 1847 had already been twice exploited by her former lover, Alexandre Dumas *fils*, in the 1848 novel and 1852 play *La Dame aux camélias*. By the time the opera was begun, the exercise was one of interpretation, translation or distillation; the achievement that of creating a character more knowable than Alphonsine, more honest than Marie, more sympathetic than Dumas's Marguerite Gautier and more potent a symbol of the great anxieties of her era:

prostitution, disease and the unstoppable appetites of a decadent, spendthrift city.

Opera has other consumptive heroines and other whores, but no character who synthesizes the terrors and temptations of her age and surroundings as gracefully and economically as Violetta Valéry. Paris, ever bigger, ever brighter, and already styled as *La Ville-Lumière*, was a centre not just of technological and commercial progress but of prostitution and medical specialism.

William Acton – whose *Prostitution, considered in its moral, social and sanitary aspects*[1] would come to be seen, somewhat unfairly, as typifying the sexual hypocrisy that caused Dumas's play to be banned in London – trained in Paris in the 1830s at the Hôpital des Vénériens du Midi, under Philippe Ricord, one of the three doctors who would consign the syphilitic Donizetti to the insane asylum in Ivry-sur-Seine in 1847. Alexandre Parent-Duchâtelet, a phrenologist-turned-hygienist, moved from the study of urban sewerage to the study of prostitution with the highly influential *De la prostitution dans la ville de Paris*.[2] Four thousand prostitutes were examined for his study, which revealed that the daughters of starch-makers, candle-makers and rag-pickers were less likely to turn to prostitution than those of coach-drivers and cobblers. Typically for his era, Parent-Duchâtelet saw one cause of prostitution as 'vanity and the desire for the glitter of luxurious clothes' (a statement echoed by Dumas in several of Marguerite's least convincing monologues). Other potential causes included a disrupted or abusive childhood and poverty. Parent-Duchâtelet's primary interest was in prostitution as an agency of communicable diseases. With the cause of consumption still unknown, he noted a coincidence between diagnoses of recto-vaginal fistulae among his case-studies and diagnoses of pulmonary consumption, but did not hazard any connection between the spread of tuberculosis and the sex industry.

As early as 1808, François-Joseph-Victor Broussais had suggested 'erotic spasms' as a possible cause of phthisis (*Histoire des phlegmasies*

---

1   London: J. Churchill, 1857.
2   Paris: J.B. Ballière, 1836.

ou inflammations chroniques).[3] In his 1819 treatise, *De l'auscultation médiate ou Traité du diagnostic des maladies des poumons et du cœur*,[4] René Laennec attributed the concentration of pulmonary tuberculosis in the city to 'bad morals' and 'syphilitic conditions'. In London, in 1839, Michael Ryan, in his *Prostitution in London, with a Comparative View of That of Paris and New York*,[5] writing of phthisis, or pulmonary tuberculosis, claimed that 'this direful and, I believe, incurable disease is often accelerated by venereal excesses'. Later, in 1852, Richard Payne Cotton, also Paris-trained, warned that 'Of all vices none are so apt as to lead to consumption as the unnatural or unrestrained indulgence of sensual passion' in *The Nature, Symptoms and Treatment of Consumption*.[6] The 1840s had seen a rash of publications centred around prostitution in various cities, though Paris remained the uncontested international capital. In Volume 1 of his moral encyclopedia *Les Français peints par eux-mêmes: Encyclopédie morale du dix-neuvième siècle* (1840–42),[7] Jules Janin echoes Parent-Duchâtelet's analysis of the cause of prostitution: 'amour de luxe, de la toilette, de la parure, c'est bien la même femme, coquette, galante, perfide, pleine de caprices'. Verdi and Piave could not have been unaware of the scholarly and more salacious interest in this subject.

While prostitution was scrutinized and bureaucratized, phthisis in the 1840s and 1850s was both familiar and widely misunderstood. A 'cult disease', consumption was, in fact, largely indiscriminate in its progress, responsible for fifty per cent of deaths under the age of twenty-five (with a slight bias towards young women), and one third of the deaths of those aged twenty-six to forty-five. From being the preserve of poets and rebels, a 'romantic death', the early symptoms of which were seen as fashionable, it was beginning to be reshaped as a 'good death' – not in the modern sense of painlessness but because the slowness of its progress afforded time for the sufferer to prepare to meet their God and atone for their sins.

---

3   Paris: Gabon, 1808.
4   Paris: Brossonet Chaudé, 1819.
5   London: H. Bailliere, 1839.
6   London: John Churchill, 1852.
7   Paris: Louis Curmer, 1840–42.

Written by a composer profoundly critical of cant and in love with a woman whose past his own family abhorred, *La traviata* does not present consumption as romantic or good. Nor does it offer much sense of redemption. *La traviata* is about fever, shortness of breath, pain, denial, bargaining, rage, resistance. Although Violetta's passing is signalled in the first, liminal notes of the score, and although we are – and always were – aware that she will die, what makes the music seduce, transcend and sear is that we too fall in love with that fallen woman.

Less coarse than Marguerite, less calculating than Alphonsine/Marie, whose teeth were famously kept clean by lying, there is a candour to Violetta that anticipates the calm gaze of Manet's 1865 *Olympia* (see 'Donna son io, signore, ed in mia casa' ('I am a lady, sir, and this is my own house'), Act Two, Scene 4). Much like Manet, Verdi hovers between intimate character study and a critique of his character's surroundings in *La traviata*. Both artists challenged the then accepted limits of taste or decency, simply because the prostitutes they depicted were plainly contemporary, as, crucially, were their clients. Had the dandies in Manet's earlier provocation *Le Déjeuner sur l'herbe* (1863) been styled as Arcadian shepherds, they would not have been consigned to the Salon des Refusés. The unspoken fear behind the rejection of the prostitute as a fit subject for a novel, a play, an opera, a painting, is one of contagion: not of consumption, but of venereal disease and moral corruption. In order to work, a whore needs customers.

Verdi was careful to include the requisite dances and drinking songs in his opera. But *La traviata* is a more modern and a more subversive work than its numbers and structure indicate. The bullfighters and gypsies at Flora's party (Act Two, Scene 10) can be heard as deliberately vacuous, modish, tinny, arch: grotesque illustrations of the city Violetta describes as a 'populous desert' (Act One, Scene 5). Among their many burdens, prostitutes were seen as symptomatic of urbanization, thus the leaving of and returning to Paris becomes of central importance in the opera, not least because it seems as though the city itself is killing (or consuming) Violetta. The carnival procession of the *bœuf gras*, heard off stage in the first scene of Act Three,

Scene 4:'Largo al quadrupede / sir della festa' ('Make way for the four-footed lord of the feast'), celebrates the imminent slaughter of one symbol of excess while we prepare to watch the death of another.

Coloratura, a necessarily artificial form of writing for the voice, is used to illustrate anxiety, recklessness, the business of living faster, as Marguerite Gautier puts it. The only shred of hysteria (another nineteenth-century medical obsession in which Paris would lead the field) is found not at the end of Act Three when Violetta experiences the phenomenon of *spes phthisica*, but in the *Allegro brillante* of 'Sempre libera degg'io' ('I must be entirely free') (Act One, Scene 5). Far from getting madder as the opera unfolds, Violetta becomes more lucid, more sober, more skilled at expressing and analysing her feelings as she nears death. Verdi's *staccato* markings suggest dyspnoea, or shortness of breath, not simply in the broken (in both senses) phrases of 'Addio del passato bei sogni ridenti' ('Farewell to those happy dreams of bygone days') in Act Three, Scene 3, but much earlier, when Alfredo's father, Germont finally makes his message clear, 'Non sapete quale affetto, / vivo, immense m'arda in petto' ('Don't you realize what a vital, / immense love burns in my heart') in Act Two. The marking here is *vivacissimo agitato*.

Violetta has two distinct rhythmic personalities: one that seizes a phrase by the upbeat (in the practised coquetry of the Act One *Brindisi*, the terrible honesty of Act Two's 'Amami, Alfredo' ('Love me, Alfredo') and the strident dread of Act Three's 'Gran Dio morir sì giovine' ('Ah! Dear God, to die so young')) and one that submits sweetly and wistfully to the downbeat 'Parigi o caro' ('My love, we shall leave Paris') in Act Three, humouring her lover, wishing it were otherwise. Having spent her life as a walking, talking, living doll, something to be shown off and displayed, like a racehorse or an expensive timepiece, she is charmed by a lover who wants instead to hide her away. By running away with Alfredo, however, she is hastening her own death according to the medical advice of the time. Can Alfredo love her as much as she loves him? No. Because his life does not depend on it.

Violetta's sacrifice is most often understood as being that of relinquishing her lover and mutely suffering his rage. Yet the voices of the doctors of her time suggest that she has already sacrificed herself by running away with him. Faking it for antique aristocrats would be less taxing than abandoning oneself to an *amant de cœur*. Dumas makes a poor argument for the sincerity of Armand Duval's love for Marguerite. In the novel, Armand is attracted, modishly, to melancholy and illness, his grandiloquent self-pity only momentarily ebbing as he stares into the empty sockets of his former lover's eyes at her exhumation. Verdi and Piave are somewhat kinder to Alfredo, though it is apparent that of the two lovers, he is the one to have benefited from their retreat to the countryside. The restless, breathless figures of 'De' miei bollenti spiriti / il giovanile ardore' ('The youthful ardour / of my passionate nature' (Act Two, Scene 1) conjure fever of the lovesick kind – curable, unlike consumption, with time. And what are we to make of Germont *père*? His reasons for insisting on the lovers' separation seem outmoded to us, and the contrast drawn between Violetta and his daughter cruel in Act Two, Scene 5 – 'Pura siccome un angelo / Iddio mi die' una figlia' ('God granted me a daughter / who is as pure as an angel') – but his analysis that this is a love that cannot last is inarguable.

The notion that chastity could prolong the life of the tuberculosis sufferer proved surprisingly durable. In Somerset Maugham's brittle romance, 'The Sanatorium',[8] the consumptive narrator is warned that his two-to-three-year life expectancy may shrink to six months if he marries his fellow patient. No mention is made of the effect on her. Equally durable was the old association between consumption and unusual beauty, though pulmonary haemorrhage, the most frequent cause of death, was never pretty, and the final stages of the disease could be disfiguring. The heroine of Maugham's story, like Violetta / Marguerite, is described as combining 'a rather curiously extreme innocence with extreme sophistication… a force of character unexpected in anyone who looked so flower-like' and enjoys the botanical name of Ivy. As ever, fact was less attractive than fiction. Mere months separated Maugham's own experience of treatment in a Scottish tuberculosis sanatorium in 1919 from the production of signs earnestly requesting passengers of the London, Brighton and

8   First published in *Cosmopolitan* magazine, December 1938.

South Coast Railway to 'abstain from the dangerous and objectionable habit of spitting'.

Kissing a consumptive, we must assume, was riskier than passing by a spittoon in the waiting room of Lewes station. Still, the romance of romancing a sickly woman persisted and mutated, never quite going away, never relaxing the pressure on casting directors to find a slim Violetta. In Barry Lategan's mid-1960s photographs of Twiggy and Corinne Day's early 1990s shots of the young Kate Moss there are faint echoes of the '*tipo traviata*', a thinness and paleness that is suggestive of ill-health. To this day, the make-up tutorial website mookychick.co.uk approvingly describes the grunge heroin chic look as 'smudgy, sexy, pale, a touch consumptive', and apocalypse heroin chic as 'still nicely consumptive'.

As Romanticism curdled into Realism, one constant remained in the nineteenth century: a fascination with the dead or dying female form. The British photographer Henry Peach Robinson contributed to this in two widely exhibited, commercially successful images, both of which used a 'perfectly healthy fourteen-year-old girl' named Miss Cundall as the model. Robinson is best known for the composite photograph *Fading Away* (1858), in which Cundall plays an idealized consumptive, expiring on a chaise longue while two female relatives watch over her and her father gazes out on a stormy cloudscape, his back turned to camera.[9] Critical reception of the picture's 'morbid and painful sentiment' echoed that of the first London run of *La traviata*. Yet demand was such that Robinson and his staff made over 200 reproductions of the image and *Fading Away* was reproduced in the November 1858 edition of *Harper's Magazine*. *She Never Told Her Love* (1857), a preliminary study for *Fading Away*, was a portrait of Miss Cundall in a similar position on the chaise longue, dying this time of heartbreak, quite alone. To the Victorian eye, lovesickness and consumption were evidently interchangeable.

The idea of death as a process of purification and beautification – of the soul, principally, but also of the body – was peddled in verse and melodrama, and reiterated in the journals and letters of

9 See Mia Fineman, *Faking It: Manipulated Photography before Photoshop* (New York: Metropolitan Museum of Art, 2012).

consumption sufferers and their relatives. The deaths of consumptives Dorothea Palmer, Elvira Horsley and Harry Goulburn as documented and analysed in Pat Jalland's study *Death in the Victorian Family*[10] indicate that maintaining that redemptive ideal required an arduous collective effort, even among the most committed Christians.

By contrast, popular culture was full of stories about fallen women jumping to their deaths in the Seine (see the widely reproduced 1880s death-mask of *L'Inconnue de la Seine*, on which the beatific face of Resussi-Annie was based), and the Thames (see Thomas Hood's 1844 poem *The Bridge of Sighs*, in which the suicide is described in typically floral, typically phthisic imagery). It was largely bunkum. As Olive Anderson's *Suicide in Victorian England*[11] reveals, parks and canals were the favoured spots for self-murder, and neither was known to improve the complexion. But it was popular and lucrative bunkum.

As high and low art slowly parted company, the First World War and the Great Depression brought a degree of gender equality to popular representations of sex-workers and with it a less condemnatory attitude. Leonello Casucci and Julius Brammer's cabaret song 'Schöner Gigolo, armer Gigolo' – a satire on economically enforced male prostitution later popularized as 'Just a Gigolo' – predates Cole Porter's 'Love for Sale' by two years. The latter (female-voiced) song was considered quite scandalous in the context of the 1930 Broadway run of Porter's musical *The New Yorkers* but found lasting success in the canon of the American Songbook. On the silver screen, vamps and tramps prevailed; Greta Garbo's aristocratic elegance in George Cukor's *Camille* (1937) sealed the deal. In Jay Presson Allen's screenplay of Muriel Spark's novella, *The Prime of Miss Jean Brodie*[12] for Ronald Neame's 1969 film of the same name, a passing reference to *La traviata* is memorably expanded to provide evidence of the frigid character of the headmistress Emmeline Mackay. ('Violetta did not expire for love of Alfredo! Violetta was a thoroughly silly woman with diseased lungs. If she'd been brought up properly, she'd have

---

10 Oxford: Oxford University Press, 1996.
11 Oxford: Clarendon Press, 1987.
12 London: Macmillan, 1961.

been out on the hockey field, breathing deeply.') Were Violetta not widely understood as deserving of sympathy by this time, the line would serve no purpose.

In the moral blur of post-feminism, Violetta's profession has become entirely secondary to her perceived independence and self-determination. If a former *Doctor Who* assistant can make trading sex for money look empowering, even enjoyable – Billie Piper in *Diary of a Call Girl* (2007–11), the television adaptation of Dr Brooke Magnanti's once anonymous blog *Belle de Jour* – the feminist discourse of exploitation and degradation is fatally undermined. In a world of S&M safe words and safe sex, the only peril Belle/Hannah faces is that of falling in love, like Violetta, Marguerite and, perhaps, Marie/Alphonsine.

The paradigm shift in popular representations of Violetta's story came with Gary Marshall's 1990 romantic comedy film *Pretty Woman*, which deftly spun several myths on femininity and prostitution into one candy-coated Cinderella story as Hollywood hooker Vivian Ward (Julia Roberts) and corporate raider Edward Lewis (Richard Gere) are cleansed and redeemed by mutual love and, significantly, ennobled by their responses to Verdi's music. In nineteenth-century terms, Vivian vaults from *femme insoumise* to *femme galante* in 119 glossy minutes. Of course, Vivian, like Alphonsine, Marie, Marguerite, and Violetta, deserves better than to be a prostitute. Her inner purity is signalled early in the movie when instead of injecting drugs in the bathroom of Edward's palatial hotel suite, she is found to be flossing her teeth. A mega-watt smile, a borrowed credit card, a new wardrobe and a crash course in etiquette enable Vivian to 'pass' as class, while the nobility of her soul is consecrated during a performance of – what else? – *La traviata*. It's an in-joke, designed to tickle those who know their Verdi. Unlike Violetta, Vivian enjoys a fairytale ending. Her renunciation of Edward is merely temporary. He rescues her, and she 'rescues him right back', while Kit, the Flora in this unsung opera, lingers in the Los Angeles *demi-monde*, dabbling with drugs, shadowed by illness.

To many women, the most memorable scene in *Pretty Woman* is not the one at the opera – it's the scene in the boutique when Vivian returns with money to burn. As the critic Carina Chocano observed in 'Thelma, Louise and All the Pretty Women',[13] *Pretty Woman* is less a love story than a money story. Downplayed in *La traviata* save for the scene at Flora's party when Alfredo throws his winnings at Violetta, money enjoys a significant role in *La Dame aux camélias*. Marguerite, like Marie, liked to spend. In a similar fashion, the affluent heroines of HBO's *Sex and the City* (1998–2004) devoted more screen-time to the acquisition of designer shoes than the pursuit of hot sex, true love or a Tiffany engagement ring. For the Indian shawls of the 1840s and 1850s, read Manolos, Jimmy Choos, Louboutins. Look at Jules Janin's 'amour de luxe' again and it seems we have barely moved on – or, if we have, we have moved straight back again.

The aggressive commercialism and pornification of popular culture, together with the near-eradication of pulmonary tuberculosis in the wealthy West – so rare has fatal TB become that when it happens it is headline news – make our relationship to *La traviata* vastly different from that experienced by nineteenth-century audiences. Few public organs or orators in Western Europe still brazenly adhere to the binary thinking of madonna versus whore, Alfredo's lover versus Alfredo's sister. But if every pretty woman can behave like a call girl – even the good women, the wives, the sisters, the mothers – what makes Violetta special? Is it just that she has, as one of Armand's acquaintances says of Marguerite, 'a few more brains and perhaps a bit more heart than the rest of them'?

In the opera, Violetta's professional life ends in the course of her first conversation with Alfredo. The past is the past, 'Più non esiste' ('It no longer exists', Act Two, Scene 5), though the last bars of Act One are inconclusive, pitching her champagne-numbed *fioritura* against his lilting promise, moving in parallel rather than together, never quite touching. Act Two is subversive, for it is not Violetta's prostitution that offends; rather, it is Violetta's desire to give up prostitution, to 'keep' and keep Alfredo. Instead of trading sex for money, she is trading money for sex, selling off the finery she has earned, her carriage and horses, her furnishings. This is an act of rebellion that the French polemicist Catherine Clément identified

---

13 *New York Times*, 21st April 2011.

as 'reversing the prostitution'.[14] What makes Violetta special? Her daring, her loss.

The end of the opera, carefully prefigured in the opening bars, is always expected, always a shock. Alfredo, should he have eluded infection, can return to Provence. His sister can marry her fiancé. Annina can find another well-connected courtesan to work for, the Baron another girl. Dr Grenvil can continue telling gentle lies to consumptives until his retirement, still some years before Robert Koch's discovery of the tubercle bacillus in 1882. And us? We can weep a little, compare our most recent experience of the opera with previous experiences, think again about the myriad of allusions to a specific time and a specific place in this tight, harsh drama, and look forward to the next performance. For Arthur Groos's suggestion that we connect to Violetta because we recognize our mortality in hers[15] is only part of it. In an opera that is about a botched love affair, bad debts and an ugly, painful death, we also have a brief connection to a moment in which love is stronger than disease, more powerful than bourgeois morality, more addictive than Indian shawls, expensive flowers and conspicuous consumption.

---

14 Cathérine Clément, *Opera, or the Undoing of Women*, trans. Betty Wing (London: Virago, 1988), p. 63.

15 '*Amore e morte*: Dying of Consumption', Royal Opera House programme, May 1998.

La traviata: A Selected Performance History

Hugo Shirley

Verdi's famous line to his student Emanuele Muzio after the unsuccessful first performance of *La traviata* has entered into operatic legend: '*La traviata*, last night, fiasco. Is it my fault or the singers'? Time will tell'.[1] The singers who took part in the premiere at Venice's famous opera house on 6th March 1853 represented something of a compromise. Giorgio Mares conducted, well enough by all accounts. The veteran baritone and old friend of Verdi's, Felice Varesi, cast as Rigoletto two years earlier, was Giorgio Germont. He was unhappy with his role in the new, unconventional work, complaining in a letter that Verdi, on this occasion, 'did not know how to use the gifts of the artists at his disposition', and about his 'adagio of an aria'. The tenor, Lodovico Graziani, was indisposed and in poor voice. Fanny Salvini-Donatelli sang Violetta well in Act One, with Tommaso Locatelli writing in the *Gazzetta ufficiale di Venezia* that she 'sang those florid passages, of which the maestro wrote her many, with an indescribable skill and perfection'. She was 'literally overwhelmed with applause', and Verdi was called out 'for a most delicate harmony

---

1   For this letter and the other quoted correspondence and reports referring to the premiere and early productions, see Fabrizio Della Seta's 'Introduction' to *La traviata*, *The Works of Giuseppe Verdi*, ed. Della Seta, vol. 19 (London, Chicago, Milan: University of Chicago Press, Ricordi, 1997), pp. xi–xxviii. For the subsequent performance history of *La traviata*, see also Thomas Kaufman, *Verdi and His Major Contemporaries: A Selected Chronology of Performances with Casts* (New York: Garland, 1990), and Alfred Loewenberg, *Annals of Opera, 1597–1940*, 3rd edn. (London: John Calder, 1978).

of the strings in the *Preludio* to the score; then for the *Brindisi*, then for the duet, then I don't know how many other times, by himself and with the prima donna, at the end of the act'.

Things went rapidly downhill during the second and third acts, however. Salvini-Donatelli soldiered on, but received inadequate support from the other principals. Applause became scarcer and, according to an account in *L'arte*: 'the big duet between Varesi and Salvini, from which Verdi expected certain success and which he declared should be the centrepiece of the opera, only elicited a little applause, disputed by some. All the rest was a *murmur*.' The dramatic effect of the whole, moreover, cannot have been helped by the fact that the censor had dictated that it was impossible to stage the opera in the present day, as Verdi repeatedly stipulated. The action, therefore, was transferred to 'the time of Richelieu', as would remain the norm for most productions over at least the next half-century.

However, the opera's brief opening run was not, recent musicology has established, quite as disastrous as Verdi, who had predicted its failure at the hands of Salvini-Donatelli and Graziani, liked to make out (the word 'fiasco' featured in several letters, with various degrees of emphasis). In retrospect we can see the soprano suffering only from the difficulties – dramatic and vocal – that have continued to plague singers of Violetta. Varesi had suggested one when he wrote to a colleague as early as November 1852 that the role would be 'poorly suited to the person of Salvini, who must interpret a being of ideal beauty in the *flower of youth*, who is wasted away and worn out by a consumption that makes her more susceptible in her emotions'. And such statements have been exaggerated so that Salvini-Donnatelli became a prototype for the sort of suspension of disbelief often required in this opera.[2] (The 1928 *Grove's Dictionary*

---

[2] The unfortunate Canadian soprano Emma Albani inspired George Bernard Shaw to a particularly barbed description of this operatic difficulty when she sang Violetta at Covent Garden in 1891, a little late in her career. The performance was already compromised by 'the maddest incongruities of furniture, costume, and manners at every turn', Shaw wrote, only to enjoy 'the crowning burlesque of a robust, joyous round-cheeked lady figuring as a moribund patient in decline'. Published in *The World*, 5th August 1891, reprinted in Shaw, *Music in London 1890–1894*, vol. 1 (London: Constable, 1956), p. 249.

of Music and Musicians description of her as 'one of the stoutest of ladies on or off the stage' seems to be a grossly unfair exaggeration.)

After the failure of the 1853 run, Verdi was intent on steering well clear of such avoidable casting problems. Entreaties from theatres wishing to stage the work were rebuffed – including one from Genoa's Teatro Carlo Felice, which was bolstered by the ill-calculated boast that they had secured the services of Salvini-Donatelli and Graziani. An approach from Rome, on the other hand, was seriously pondered, until reports of the singers lined up for it proved unsatisfactory and the proposed censorship too much: 'They made la traviata *pure and innocent*,' exclaimed Verdi in a letter. 'A *whore* must always be a *whore*.'

Productions in Bergamo and Naples were also rejected, with Venice's Teatro San Benedetto finally agreed upon as the site for *La traviata*'s second chance, with a cast of better-suited principals and top-class comprimarios. Verdi made various adjustments, including to Germont *père*'s tessitura, to accommodate the vocal range of the baritone Filippo Coletti. 'After a year, I have carefully examined this poor Traviata with a cool mind, and I persist in thinking that she is not such a bad devil as she was made out,' he wrote to Vigna, reiterating, however, that 'everything depends, I think, on the prima donna'. Happily, that prima donna, Maria Spezia, would prove equal to the task. At the end of rehearsals, Piave wrote to Ricordi: 'I have the satisfaction of telling you that Spezia is made for this opera, and that this opera seems made for Spezia.' In a postscript, he added that Coletti and the tenor, Francesco Landi, 'are above praise, and in a word I tell you that the whole opera from beginning to end seems a different, more sublime one than that of La Fenice'. The revival was conducted by Carlo Ercole Bosoni and used the spruced-up costumes from La Fenice, with Piave in charge of stage movement and scenery by Giuseppe Bertoia again.

The first night, on 6th May, was an unqualified triumph. '*La traviata*,' Locatelli wrote anonymously in the *Gazetta ufficiale di Venezia* the next day, 'vilified and downtrodden at La Fenice, rose, deservedly, to the stars at Gallo's Teatro San Benedetto.' He continued: 'To speak of Spezia in *La traviata*, one must employ the phrases

used for Pasta in *Norma*, or for Malibran in [Rossini's] *Otello*.'
For Landi, as Alfredo, to have performed 'with greater intelligence
and good taste would be impossible', while Coletti made the role
of Germont understandable: the character's 'motif, that famous
"Di Provenza il mare, il suol", until now only a caricature, here appears in all its splendour.' Ricordi wrote proudly to the composer,
'I must repeat to you that there never was an example in Venice of
a success equal to that of *La traviata* [...] Gallo writes to me that
the third evening was a pandemonium of applause.' Girolamo Cerri
noted, referring to Verdi's own reaction to the first night, that 'time
has told' where and with whom fault for the initial failure lay. But
Verdi, too, was keen to emphasize, somewhat disingenuously and
inaccurately, that, despite reports to the contrary, 'the *Traviata* now
being performed at San Benedetto is the same, the very same as
was performed last year at La Fenice, with the exception of a few
transpositions and a few *puntature*'. The adjustments were slightly
more significant than that.

In this revised form, and with such an overwhelming triumph
under its belt, the new *La traviata*'s progress was unstoppable, if still
impeded in Italy by the scruples of the censors: a version performed
at Rome's Teatro Apollo on 30th December 1854 was, in the words
of Fabrizio Della Seta, the editor of the critical edition of the score,
'an infamous parody of the original drama'.[3] Attempts to persuade
Spezia to sing the role again in Italy before she departed on a tour
to Spain were fruitless ('Perhaps she's expecting,' a piqued Ricordi
wrote to Verdi), and its first revivals were in Florence and Rovigo
in September and October, with two important early Violettas –
Virginia Boccadabati and Adelaide Cortesi respectively – who would
be responsible for many performances around Italy. The opera's
progress outside of Italy was speedy and wide-reaching. 1855 saw
La traviata performed in Barcelona, Malta, Vienna (4th May, at the
Kärntnertortheater; in the same day's *Die Presse*, Eduard Hanslick
wrote, 'Consumptive like the opera's heroine, Verdi's music retains
interest only insofar as it intermittently suffers from delirium tremens.
The music is of such tediousness that it practically amounts to an

---

3   Della Seta, 'Introduction', p. xxvii.

assassination'[4]), and Rio de Janeiro (its first western-hemisphere performance, at the Teatro Fluminense on 15th December), as well as Madrid, Cadiz and Lisbon, as part of Spezia's tour. In 1856 it made it to London, Buenos Aires, Warsaw, Moscow, Dublin, Mexico, Paris and New York; in 1857 it ventured further around the United States, to Cincinnati, Boston, New Orleans and Philadelphia. Before the work was a decade old, it had been seen in Italian in Santiago de Chile, Montevideo, Bucharest, Zagreb, Corsica, Amsterdam, Berlin, Brussels; in the vernacular in Budapest, Hamburg and Melbourne; as well as in Milwaukee and Prague in German versions. By the close of the century, Violetta had met her end in Croatian, Swedish, Russian, Polish, Finnish, Danish and Slovenian too, and in five other languages by 1923, when *La traviata* was performed in Hebrew in Tel Aviv, apparently the first opera to be so.

A few further statistics go to show quite how popular *La traviata* has been. Indeed, its tally of some 460 performances at Covent Garden at the time of writing seems rather paltry compared with the 793 performances totted up at the Metropolitan Opera in New York between 1883 and 1985, and over 650 accumulated at the Vienna Hof- and Staatsoper by the end of the last millennium. Perhaps surprisingly, its popularity is no less overwhelming in Germany, even though it took rather longer to reach the important German houses after its premiere than many of Verdi's other works (according to some statistics, it took an average of twenty years to reach the main German stages compared to *Il trovatore*'s five).[5] Nevertheless, it managed to reach 601 performances at the Berlin Hof- and later Staatsoper between 1860 and 1952 (only a dozen fewer than Wagner's *Der fliegende Holländer* managed in a 108-year period) and 666 at the Hamburg Opera between 1857 and 1977 (more than Mozart's *Die Entführung aus dem Serail* had achieved in the first 190 years since its first performance there). Meanwhile, according to statistics

---

4   Extract reprinted in the programme for *La traviata*, Wiener Staatsoper (1992), p. 50.

5   See the table accompanying Klaus Hortschansky, 'Die Herausbildung eines deutschsprachigen Verdi-Repertoires im 19. Jahrhundert und die zeitgenössische Kritik', *Analecta musicologica*, 11 (1972), pp. 140–84.

from Operabase.com, in the five seasons up to and including that of 2011–12, there were more performances of *La traviata* worldwide than of any other opera: with a total of 629, it easily beat both *La bohème* (580) and *Carmen* (573). With its popularity speedily and firmly established, *La traviata* sailed serenely through wildly changing operatic climates, remaining, like its middle-period stablemates *Il trovatore* and *Rigoletto*, largely unaffected by the trends and renaissances that have dictated the fortunes of many other of Verdi's works.

Given that *La traviata* is an opera so focused on its protagonist, much of its early history can – and should – be told through its Violettas. To do so, though, one should acknowledge that very few of the great sopranos through the late nineteenth and twentieth centuries have not tackled the role at some stage, even though, as Lanfranco Rasponi notes in *The Last Prima Donnas*, 'none of them can possibly do it complete justice'. He goes on: 'Lyrics, spintos and dramatics encounter their share of difficulties in the perplexing agility demanded by the first act, and coloraturas begin having their troubles in the second act, which demands much more emotional impact [...] Needless to say, many of them must have the first-act scena lowered by a half-tone or an entire tone, and even then the "Sempre libera" is a holy terror.'[6] Only a small fraction of history's Violettas can reasonably be covered here, but those already mentioned played their part in the opera's further dissemination. Spezia, once back from her Iberian tour, sang the role at the first Milan performance (in September 1856 at the Teatro alla Canobbiana). A chastened Salvini-Donatelli would even reprise the role, albeit only on a trio of lesser stages. But another soprano, a descendant of the same old Italian family that had produced Pope Pius II, Marietta Piccolomini, would be instrumental in spreading *La traviata* around Europe. She, like Spezia, was later thought of as a potential Cordelia for Verdi's projected *Re Lear*, and first sang Violetta in Turin in November 1855 (at the Teatro Carignano) before becoming the toast of the Sienese Carnival season with the role the next year.

---

6   Lanfranco Rasponi, *The Last Prima Donnas* (London: Gollancz, 1984), p. 19.

Piccolomini introduced *La traviata* to London, at Her Majesty's Theatre on 24th May 1856 (Covent Garden was temporarily out of action, having burnt down a couple of months earlier). Her co-stars were Enrico Calzolari (Alfredo) and Federico Beneventano Del Bosco (Germont), and the opera created an immediate furore, thrown headlong into contemporary debates about (im)morality on the stage. (A *Times* editorial on 9th August 1856 felt the need for 'indignant protest against this exhibition of harlotry – whether harlotry triumphant, or harlotry repentant – upon the public stage'.[7]) Two years later, *La traviata* was first performed at Covent Garden (on 25th May 1858, with Angiolina Bosio, Italo Gardoni and Francesco Graziani, conducted by Michael Costa), but in the meantime it was Piccolomini who had introduced it to Birmingham, Manchester, Liverpool and Dublin, as well as Paris, at the Théâtre des Italiens, in a performance unauthorized by the composer, and which he tried in vain to stop. A later version, *Violetta*, divided into four acts and with a text by Édouard Duprez, would establish itself at Léon Carvalho's Théâtre-Lyrique-Impérial. Unveiled on 27th October 1864, it featured Christina Nilsson as Violetta. Theories that Verdi had something to do with the adjustments of this edition, however, are now thought to be unfounded; but he approved it, or at least was happy with it. (This new edition included the option to excise Germont's cabaletta after 'Di Provenza', one of the usual cuts introduced throughout *La traviata*'s history which it has only recently become standard practice to restore.)

After the opera made it to North America on 3rd December 1856, where it was performed at the Academy of Music in New York, several early American performances were met with either a lack of enthusiasm or familiar expressions of moral outrage. When it made it to Chicago in a 1859 season organized by Amalia Patti (Adelina's sister) and her husband Maurice Strakosch, it prompted a writer in the city's *Daily Journal* to place Verdi's work in exalted company: 'To be sure, we must atone during Lent for witnessing *Traviata*… and *Don Juan*, with their lax morals not altogether covered up by

---

7 For the controversy that raged in *The Times*, see George Hall, 'The Apotheosis of Prostitution', in the programme for *La traviata*, Royal Opera House (2011–12 season), pp. 37–40.

the divine music of the masters.'[8] When it was presented for the first time in San Francisco (on 13th August 1859, at the American Theatre with the husband-and-wife team of Giovanna and Eugenio Bianchi), critics seemed a little puzzled, but the *Daily Evening Bulletin* admitted that it was 'a great work and should be heard by everyone'.[9]

While Violetta would be a calling card for Adelina Patti herself, it was the so-called 'Polish Patti', Marcella Sembrich, who introduced *La traviata* to New York's Metropolitan Opera in the house's inaugural season (5th November 1883, with Victor Capoul and Giuseppe Del Puente as Alfredo and Germont, conducted by Augusto Vianesi). One of the Met's next important Violettas was the American soprano Lillian Nordica, who first sang the role there on December 1894, having sung it first in Italy some fifteen years earlier and in 1887 at Covent Garden. She was unusual in being a singer of a more dramatic sort: a year after her Met *La traviata* she would be singing Isolde in the same house.

Of Patti's many performances, one demands particular mention: her famous farewell appearance at Covent Garden in the role on 11th June 1895. She was joined by Fernando De Lucia and Mario Ancona, and Luigi Mancinelli conducted; but media interest seemed concentrated on Patti's idea of having the corsage of her dress for the Act Three ball scene studded with diamonds taken from her finest jewels. 'Tomorrow night,' the *Daily News* wrote, 'another opportunity will be afforded at the opera of seeing the Patti costumes and the Patti diamonds, which in *La traviata* last Tuesday shared the honours with Mme Patti's singing.' Their value (estimated in 1920 as £200,000), the article continues, 'has rendered necessary certain precautions at the opera house, where a couple of individuals not wholly unknown at the Bow Street establishment opposite silently figure among Violetta's guests'.[10]

---

8 Quoted in Ronald Davis, *Opera in Chicago* (New York: Appleton-Century, 1966), p. 13.

9 Quoted in George Martin, *Verdi at the Golden Gate: Opera and San Francisco in the Gold Rush Years* (Berkeley, Los Angeles and London: University of California Press, 1993), p. 144.

10 Quoted in Herman Klein, *The Reign of Patti* (1920, repr. New York: Arno Press, 1977), p. 328.

Another famous Violetta, Luisa Tetrazzini, whose performances in the role had been seen on an Argentinian tour in the 1890s, and as far afield as Kiev and Tbilisi in 1901, came unheralded to Covent Garden on 2nd November 1907 (with Fernando Carpi and Mario Sammarco, conducted by Ettore Panizza). Few knew of her reputation, but a half-empty auditorium filled up as the performance progressed and word spread. A review in the *Daily Mail*, however, hints at the esteem in which Verdi's opera – still viewed very much as a diva vehicle – was held: she brought to the role 'a human tenderness and a pathos few of us realized that it possessed'.[11] Tetrazzini returned to Covent Garden every year until 1912, appearing opposite John McCormack, who also sang Alfredo opposite Dame Nellie Melba on several occasions in the house. And, as well as appearances together at the Met (in November 1910), Melba and McCormack starred together in the roles in Australia (Caruso, originally envisaged as Melba's partner on the tour, was unwilling to commit to the necessary travel). The impresario James Cassius Williamson imported wholesale a company of some 200 members, and their *La traviata* opened to wild acclaim on 2nd September 1911 at Sydney's Her Majesty's Theatre (the conductor was Thomas Quinlan), before heading to Melbourne.

La traviata's advance into the twentieth century was further aided by technological innovations. Extracts from the opera began to proliferate in the new medium of sound recording. It was a tenor, surprisingly, who was the first to record an extract, Ferruccio Giannini setting down his take on 'Dei miei bollenti spiriti' in 1899. Other early oddities included a retired Geraldine Farrar (a Violetta at the Met opposite Caruso in 1908) accompanying herself ('horribly', according to Alan Jefferson in *Opera*) on the piano through Violetta's Act One scene, and Mary Garden, Debussy's first Mélisande, tackling 'Di Provenza il mar'.[12] Cinema also began to play a role in popularizing, if not Verdi's at first, then at least Dumas's heroine, with

---

11 Quoted in Charles Neilson Gattey, *Luisa Tetrazzini: The Florentine Nightingale* (Aldershot: The Scolar Press, 1994), p. 73.

12 See Alan Jefferson 'Opera on the Gramophone: 33 – "*La traviata*" Part 1', in *Opera* (June 1972), pp. 504–12.

some ten adaptations of his play produced in the first two decades of the century, including one starring Sarah Bernhardt (*La Dame aux camélias*, 1911); another featured Rudolph Valentino and Alla Nazimova (*Camille*, 1921).

The early twentieth century additionally saw developments in acting for the opera stage, in part attributed to the influence of such actresses as Eleonora Duse, briefly romantically attached to Verdi's librettist Arrigo Boito, and highly regarded for her portrayal of the heroine in Dumas's play. With the concomitant arrival of *verismo* in the 1890s, so arrived a different sort of Violetta. Gemma Bellincioni, who created the role of Santuzza in *Cavalleria rusticana* in 1890, was one of these, admired by Verdi when she sang in *La traviata* at La Scala in 1886 (she was the first to wear a nineteenth-century crinoline for the role, and Verdi remarked in a letter that she 'brought new life to the old sinner'[13]). Rosina Storchio, Puccini's first Butterfly, was another, and performed in an important new production at La Scala in 1906, which opened on 27th January. Leonid Sobinov was Alfredo, and Riccardo Stracciari (who would join Sembrich and Caruso in the opera at the Met in December) played his father. Leopoldo Mugnone conducted, but the novelty came in the scenery and costumes, which for once abandoned the seventeenth century and embraced, half a century late, the 'contemporary' 1850s.

For Amelita Galli-Curci's Met debut (14th November 1921), meanwhile, the émigré Jugendstil architect Joseph Urban (made famous in New York for his designs for the Ziegfeld Follies) provided lavish designs. The conductor was Roberto Moranzoni and the cast featured two legendary names as Germont father and son: Giuseppe de Luca and Beniamino Gigli. Galli-Curci represented for some a final flourish of the light-voiced 'nightingale' Violetta. By contrast, Claudia Muzio represented a refinement of the newer sort, as her striking recordings of extracts of the role demonstrate; speculation as to the cause of her own early death, meanwhile, includes the suggestion that she died of tuberculosis, giving her Violetta a certain

---

13 Quoted in John Warrack and Ewan West (eds.), *The Concise Oxford Dictionary of Opera*, 3rd edn. (Oxford and New York: Oxford University Press, 1996), p. 41.

posthumous authenticity. She also starred in the first production to be staged in 'modern' dress, at Rome's Teatro dell'Opera on 19th April 1928. Ezio Cellini was the director, Alessandro Magnoni provided the sets and Ileana Leonidov conducted. Joining Muzio in the cast were Tito Schipa and Stracciari. Another important inter-war Violetta who deserves mention is Rosa Ponselle, who sang rarely but to enormous acclaim: at Covent Garden, just six times in 1930–31, and at the Met in 1931 and 1934.

Among the most notable performances during the war was a new, double-cast production that opened at the Vienna Staatsoper on 19th December 1940. It was conducted by Leopold Ludwig, with the director-designer team of Oscar Fritz Schuh and Caspar Neher and, as one of the Alfredos, Anton Dermota. With other Verdi operas adjusted to fit the ideological needs of the Third Reich, *La traviata*'s general popularity in Austria and Germany (where it was usually sung in German) seems to have remained largely unaffected: the opera was either seen as entertainment of a more frivolous – and therefore harmless – sort, or as conveniently containing a cautionary lesson regarding the moral laxity – and therefore degeneracy – of the French. After the destruction of the Staatsoper in Vienna, Schuh staged a new version in the Theater an der Wien on 27th February 1947. Josef Krips conducted, the opera was sung in Italian, and Dermota was joined in the cast by Elisabeth Schwarzkopf and Giuseppe Taddei. In wartime Britain, meanwhile, Sadler's Wells Opera's 1940 tour consisted of *La traviata* and *Le nozze di Figaro*, using the same basic set for each. Joan Cross, who later took over the management of the company, was Violetta. Tyrone Guthrie directed a new, if still modest staging (with designs by Sophie Fedorovitch) at the New Theatre in 1943, in which Peter Pears sang Alfredo. Cross, for many UK critics one of the great Violettas, would go on to direct her own production of *La traviata* at Sadler's Wells in 1950, with sets by William Chappell and a cast made up of Victoria Shires, Rowland Jones and Arnold Matters.

Across the Atlantic, the immediate post-war period saw Arturo Toscanini going some way to reclaiming the purely musical integrity of Verdi's score with his 1946 recording of the work, with a cast of Met stars – Licia Albanese, Jan Peerce and Robert Merrill – and his NBC Symphony Orchestra. But if Toscanini had shifted the focus momentarily away from the soprano back onto the conductor and composer, the limelight would soon be wrested back by Maria Callas, whose reign as the pre-eminent post-war Violetta coincided with a staging of the opera that might be seen to mark the start of *La traviata*'s love-hate relationship with 'the Age of the Producer'.[14] She starred in the Luchino Visconti production that opened at La Scala on 28th May 1955. Giuseppe di Stefano and Ettore Bastianini sang the Germonts; Carlo Maria Giulini conducted. Visconti updated the action to the end of the nineteenth century, with Lila de Nobili designing the sets, as well as the costumes, in which Visconti aimed to give the recently slimmed-down Callas 'a little of Duse, a little of Rachel and a little of Bernhardt'. The production and her performance, he had explained to Callas's husband, 'should represent... her aim, her interpretative masterpiece, her artistic culmination, her Ninth Symphony'.[15] It also represented a breakthrough: 'Today Visconti's production might seem a modest gesture in the direction of realism,' the Callas biographer Michael Scott has written, 'yet its appearance was of a beauty... that had certainly not been equalled until then; and it became a precursor of countless *La traviata*s.'[16]

When the Callas rival Joan Sutherland sang Violetta at Covent Garden for the first time, by contrast, it was in an old production with designs by Sophie Fedorovitch. With Callas's own 1958 London performances fresh in the memory, *The Times* noted that 'Much of [Sutherland's] acting was characterless', pointing out that 'Covent

---

14 Harold Rosenthal's review in *Opera* (June 1967), pp. 512–16, of Visconti's 1967 Royal Opera production complained that 'it certainly seemed, at first sight, as if what I called in my recent book on Covent Garden, the Age of the Producer, is still very much with us'. That recent book was *Opera at Covent Garden: A Short History* (London: Gollancz, 1967), whose third part was entitled, 'The Age of the Producer, 1945–?'. The question mark remains appropriate.

15 Giovanni Battista Meneghini, *Maria Callas mia moglie* (Milan: Rusconi, 1981), p. 182, quoted in Michael Scott, *Maria Meneghini Callas* (London: Simon & Schuster, 1991), p. 152.

16 Scott, *Callas*, p. 153.

Garden had not the courage to name a producer for this revival.'[17] Otto Klemperer, who popped in to watch a single act of Sutherland's performance, was a little more succinct in a letter to his daughter on 23rd January 1960: 'an extraordinarily beautiful voice and an extraordinarily bad actress'.[18] Sutherland would also sing Violetta on a legendary tour to Australia, with a young Luciano Pavarotti, in 1965. And their *Traviata* together in Sydney in 1965 saw various strands of performance history coming together. Sutherland had been presented with a pen that Melba had used to write Violetta's letter in the same city in 1924, and used it in her performance while also wearing a necklace of gold camellias that had belonged to Duse, also lent to Sutherland for the occasion.

Covent Garden got its new production just a couple of years later, from Visconti. When it opened on 19th April 1967 (with Giulini again conducting, and a cast made up of Mirella Freni, Renato Cioni and Piero Cappuccilli, with sets by Nato Frasca and costumes by Vera Mazot), Harold Rosenthal noted in *Opera* (June 1967) that 'it was, for reasons best known to Visconti, updated to the end of the nineteenth century and set... in black and white *à la* Beardsley'. Despite acknowledging the production's effectiveness – and praising above all Giulini's conducting – he concluded by asking, 'How will this production wear? I'm sure we will soon tire of the black and white sets.' (In the event, the production lasted at Covent Garden until 1986.) There was rather more praise for the production John Copley unveiled at Sadler's Wells Opera at the London Coliseum on 14th March 1973. Josephine Barstow, John Brecknock and Geoffrey Chard were the three principals, David Walker designed the sets and Nicholas Braithwaite conducted. The same production was to herald, on 3rd August 1974, the first Coliseum performance of English National Opera, as Sadler's Wells Opera had been renamed. On that occasion, the principals were Valerie Masterson, Keith Erwen and Norman Bailey; Charles Mackerras conducted. Masterson headed

17 Quoted in Brian Adams, *La Stupenda: A Biography of Joan Sutherland* (London: Hutchinson, 1981), p. 107.
18 Peter Heyworth, *Klemperer: His Life and Times*, vol. 2 (Cambridge: Cambridge University Press, 1996), p. 281.

a slightly different cast, also under Mackerras and with the ENO Orchestra and Chorus, that was recorded too, and an important new production in Munich the following year formed the basis of another recording. The traditional staging was by Otto Schenk and designed by Jürgen Rose, the Violetta was Ileana Cotrubas and the conductor was Carlos Kleiber. It opened on 26th April 1975, Giacomo Aragall and Wolfgang Brendel were the Germonts; but when Kleiber recorded the work with Cotrubas, one of the most admired Violettas of her generation, for Deutsche Grammophon in 1976–77, she was joined by Plácido Domingo and Sherrill Milnes.

Domingo would also star, with Teresa Stratas and Cornell MacNeil, in a lavish film version of the opera (released internationally in 1983) directed by Franco Zeffirelli, with costume designs by Piero Tosi and cinematography by Ennio Guanieri. In its detail and cinematic cohesion, it also easily outgunned previous film versions by Carmine Gallone (1947) and Mario Lanfranchi (1968), even if the latter starred another great Violetta, Anna Moffo. But by the time of the next film version, a rather coolly received affair directed for television by Pierre Cavassilas in 2000, and starring Eteri Gvazava, José Cura and Rolando Panerai, productions of the opera in the theatre had moved on a great deal.

At Covent Garden, a new Royal Opera production by Richard Eyre and with designs by Bob Crowley successfully brought a modern look to a 'period' conception (and is still going strong at the time of writing). Georg Solti conducted, and his influence, allied to his admiration for the twenty-nine-year-old Romanian soprano singing her first Violetta in the production, led to the BBC clearing one of its channel's evening schedules and broadcasting the opening night live on TV on 25th November 1994. That soprano was Angela Gheorghiu, who was joined by Frank Lopardo and Leo Nucci. The grand-scale period realism of Eyre's production was successful in a way that Jonathan Miller's new ENO production unveiled on 12th September 1996 was not, proving the difficulty of balancing a basically conservative aesthetic with the dramatic persuasiveness that was increasingly expected. In sets by Bernard Culshaw and costumes by Clare Mitchell,

Miller's production was deemed to lack the grandeur and luxury many felt necessary.

Both London productions contrasted with developments elsewhere, and in February 1993 Klaus Michael Grüber had experimented with something altogether more abstract in Paris's Théâtre du Châtelet (designs by Lucio Fanti). With support from the Philharmonia (on a month's residency) and Antonio Pappano, the cast of Verónica Villarroel, Jean-Luc Viala and David Pittman-Jennings seems to have struggled to get to the heart of the opera – Joel Kasow in *Opera* (May 1993) wrote of 'a gaping hole at the centre' and Villerroel 'having the emotional projection of an amoeba'. There was more abstraction in Günter Krämer's new Bayerische Staatsoper production in Munich later that year. Designed by Andreas Reinhardt, it was described by Beate Kayser at the time (again in *Opera*, in the 1993 Festivals issue), as 'logical, bleak and a bit cold', and unflinchingly focused on its Violetta (in this case Julia Varady), whose death became more than ever a grim spectacle for a voyeuristic, celebrity-obsessed audience.

Yet more experimentation came in Harry Kupfer's 1995 staging for Berlin's Komische Oper, whose single set (by Hans Schavernoch) reproduced some sort of subterranean space – in *Opera* (May 1995), Barry Emslie couldn't tell whether it was 'a Parisian Metro without rails or a sewer without water' – in which the opera's events were played out as a flashback in Violetta's mind. Another 'concept' production (again, the scare quotes seem to be employed with special disapproval with this work) appeared in late 1999 at the Canadian Opera Company, by the Russian director Dmitry Bertman. It featured sets by Igor Nezhny, costumes by Tatiana Tulubieva and a cast made up of Zvetelina Vassileva, Vladimir Grishko and Gaétan Laperrière. This time, the concept seems to have been built around the power of contrasts, but reportedly suffered from distracting additional action. A more fundamental problem, however, was one that all updatings of *La traviata* have to address: the opera's drama relies on the existence of a social hierarchy, with attendant expectations and prejudices, which an escape into the abstract cannot be relied upon to make up for.

Peter Mussbach's 2003 staging at the Berlin Staatsoper was more successful in its abstract approach than some, however, partly because of the musical performance, with Daniel Barenboim making an excursion into the Italian repertory. There was no set to speak of, and the only props were chairs, while what little dramatic action there was remained contained, as was the orchestra, behind a gauze curtain onto which images could be projected. Rolando Villazón and Thomas Hampson were the Germonts, and Christine Schäfer, clad in a white dress that signified Violetta as much as the singer herself, became, according again to Barry Emslie in *Opera* (July 2003), 'a "figure" who transcends convention and becomes a vibrant aesthetic creation'. One of the images projected onto the gauze in Mussbach's production was of a large clock, and it was an oversize clock that would be the central image in Willy Decker's 2005 modern-dress staging at the Salzburg Festival (designed by Wolfgang Gussmann): an effective compromise between a non-specific, semi-abstract location and unashamedly realistic *Personenregie*. Villazón and Hampson played the Germonts again, this time alongside Anna Netrebko's Violetta. The clock underlined the character's mortality, while Dr Grenvil hovered around the action as an enigmatic father figure. Such symbolism effectively counteracted the vagueness of the society and Violetta's position within it in a way that two more recent modern-day productions – by Jean-François Sivadier at Aix-en-Provence (July 2011, with Natalie Dessay, Charles Castronovo and Ludovic Tézier) and Deborah Warner's at the Theater an der Wien (May 2012, with Irina Lungu, Saimir Pirgu and Gabriele Viviani) – arguably failed to do, even though Warner opted, like Decker, to have a father-like figure look over Violetta throughout.

But more specificity also causes problems. Robert Carsen updated the action of the opera for the (slightly delayed) 150th anniversary of its premiere, at the newly renovated La Fenice on 12th November 2004. With designs by Patrick Kinmonth, he showed Violetta as a modern call girl. It was a 'basic error', according to Max Loppert in *Opera* (February 2005), 'since after all Violetta is a courtesan, a kept woman, not a Heidi Fleiss hooker'. The interest of hearing the score performed as it was first presented at La Fenice in 1853, meanwhile, seems to have been counteracted by the conducting of Lorin Maazel. For the Opéra de Paris in June 2007, Christoph Marthaler (with designs by Anna Viebrock, and a cast of Christine Schäfer, Jonas Kaufmann and José van Dam) chose specific references to an Edith Piaf of the mid-1950s (when the singer was known to have had drug issues), but resorted in the end, according to Warwick Thompson, again in *Opera* (September 2007), to 'the hoary "theatre-as-life" metaphor so beloved of directors with nothing to say'.

Jürgen Flimm's 2005 Zurich Opera Festival staging (with sets by Erich Wonder) took the action back to the *fin de siècle* once more, in a production that, in the words of George Hall reviewing the DVD release (*Opera*, May 2006), was 'fairly traditional, even conventional', but which ended up 'too vague and unspecific when it comes down to essentials'. More recently, and more successfully, David McVicar's October 2008 Scottish Opera production took the action further back, to the 1880s. In a single set by Tanya McCallin, McVicar showed that, above all, *La traviata* is an opera that reacts positively to detailed direction and fine acting, in this case from Carmen Giannattasio, Federico Lepre and Richard Zeller; Emmanuel Joel-Hornak conducted.

More recently, *La traviata* has been subjected to large-scale treatments that might seem surprising for an opera in which, unusually, every scene takes place indoors. Graham Vick's 2004 production at the vast Arena di Verona (with designs by Paul Brown) was dismissed by Max Loppert in *Opera* (November 2004) as 'a horror of ill-digested thought-process, claptrap dramaturgy and cack-handed stagecraft'. It did, however, apparently have the distinction of being the 'Princess Diana *Traviata*', the late royal becoming the latest modern-day addition to the roll-call of the female fallen. The same director's production with his community-based Birmingham Opera Company at the similarly sized National Indoor Arena in 2007 (with sets by Paul Brown, featuring a giant doll in Act One) was much more favourably received, and featured Talise Trevigne's Violetta, at the head of a 300-strong cast, as a modern celebrity. The following year, Zurich Opera and the Swiss broadcaster SF1 staged a live TV version of the opera from among the bustling crowds in the city's main railway station. In 2012, meanwhile, the opera was staged by Opera Australia on a special barge in Sydney harbour. Francesca Zambello's production (in a vast set designed by Brian Thomson) featured an enormous chorus, an orchestra hidden underneath the stage, and cast made up of Emma Matthews, Gianluca Terranova and Jonathan Summers. The centrepiece of the production was a 3.5 tonne chandelier. Affectionately nicknamed 'Chandy', it was made up of over 11,000 sparkling crystals: Patti would surely have approved.

Throughout its history *La traviata* has shown itself resilient in the face of an enormous variety of approaches, even if it is a work with a sort of inbuilt self-righting mechanism that, whatever emphasis a director might choose, forces the dramatic focus back onto the protagonist and her personal tragedy. We like to imagine society has moved on since the 1850s, but it still, arguably, contains enough hypocrisy to produce a steady stream of modern-day Violettas to be mapped onto Verdi's heroine. But perhaps Peter Konwitschny's Oper Graz production, which opened in the Austrian city in March 2011 and transferred to ENO and the Coliseum little under two years later for the Verdi bicentenary, with Corinne Winters in the title role, marks one new departure that subsequent productions will try to emulate. In Johannes Leiacker's designs, it made additional cuts to Verdi's score and opted for a new kind of abstract updating that avoided specific references to create, as Konwitschny explained in an interview accompanying the DVD release of the original production from Graz, 'a surrealistic, indeed nightmarish world, of symbolic theatre'. It emphasized Violetta's ostracism by emotionally incapable men, and, instead of a love story, centred on 'the story of a woman who has learnt that she is going to die soon and refuses to accept the fact'.[19] And while experimental productions of *La traviata* attract more opprobrium than similar productions of most other operas, it is a work that can surely sustain a variety of approaches. Indeed, it demands them lest we forget quite how progressive Verdi's conception was.

---

19 ' "Daring to an extreme": Peter Konwitschny talks to Bernd Krispin about the Graz production of *La traviata*', booklet accompanying Verdi, *La traviata*, Arthaus DVD 101587/Blu-ray 108386, pp. 7–9.

Thematic Guide

Themes from the opera have been identified by the numbers in square brackets in the articles. These are printed at corresponding points in the libretto, so that the words can be related to the musical themes.

The critical edition of *La traviata*, edited by Fabrizio Della Seta and published by Ricordi/University of Chicago Press, appeared in 1996. For the first time it offers performers and scholars an edition of the opera based on Verdi's autograph score; it also supplies (as appendix material) the version of the opera that was performed at the La Fenice premiere, before Verdi revised the score after its hostile reception there. The music examples printed here are all in accordance with this critical edition.

[13] **VIOLETTA**

Vivacissimo

Non sa - pe - te   qua-le af-fet - to   vi-vo im- men- so__ m'ar-de il pet - to!

[14] **VIOLETTA**

Andantino cantabile

Di - te al - la   gio - vi-ne   si   bel - la e   pu - ra,

[15]

Adagio

[16] **VIOLETTA**

Allegro assai mosso

A   ma - mi, Al - fre - do

[17] **GERMONT**

Andante piuttosto mosso

Di Pro - ven-za il mar, il suol, chi dal   cor ti can-cel - lò?

[18]

Allegro brillante

[19] **CHORUS**

Allegro moderato

Noi sia - mo   zin-ga - rel - le ve-nu - te   da lon - ta - no;

[20] **CHORUS**

Allegro assai vivo

È____ Pi - quil - lo un bel____ ga - gliar - do

71

[28] **ALFREDO**

Andante mosso

Pa - ri - gi, o ca - ra, noi___ la - sce - re - mo,

[28a]

[29] **VIOLETTA**

Allegro

Gran Dio! Mo - rir sì gio - vi - ne, io che pe - na - to ho tan - to!

[30] **VIOLETTA**

Andante

Se u - na pu - di - ca ver - gi - ne

73

La traviata

Opera in three acts
by Giuseppe Verdi

Libretto by Francesco Maria Piave
after the play *La Dame aux camélias* by Alexandre Dumas *fils*

English translation by Andrew Huth

La traviata was first performed at the Teatro La Fenice, Venice, on 6th March 1853. It was first performed in Britain at Her Majesty's Theatre, London, on 24th May 1856. The first performance in the United States was at the Academy of Music, New York, on 3rd December 1856.

THE CHARACTERS

Violetta Valéry *a courtesan*	soprano
Flora Bervoix *her friend*	mezzo-soprano
Baron Douphol *Violetta's protector*	baritone
Marquis D'Obigny *friend of Flora*	bass
Doctor Grenvil	bass
Gaston, Vicomte de Létorières	tenor
Alfredo Germont	tenor
Annina *Violetta's maid*	soprano
Giuseppe *Violetta's servant*	tenor
Giorgio Germont *Alfredo's father*	baritone
Servant to Flora	bass
Messenger	bass

Ladies and gentlemen, friends of Violetta and Flora, matadors, picadors, gypsies, servants of Violetta and Flora, masquers, dancers

Paris and its environs

ATTO PRIMO

Preludio [1, 16]

Scena I

Parigi, nel 1850 circa. Salotto in casa di Violetta. Nel fondo è la porta che mette ad altra sala; ve ne sono altre due laterali; a sinistra un caminetto con sopra uno specchio. Nel mezzo è una tavola riccamente imbandita.

(Violetta, seduta sopra un divano, sta discorrendo col Dottore e con alcuni amici, mentre altri vanno ad incontrare quelli che sopraggiungono, tra i quali sono il Barone e Flora al braccio del Marchese.) [2]

INVITI I
Dell'invito trascorsa è già l'ora…
Voi tardaste…

INVITI II
Giocammo da Flora,
e giocando quell'ore volar.

VIOLETTA *(Va loro incontro.)*
Flora, amici, la notte che resta
d'altre gioie qui fate brillar…
Fra le tazze più viva è la festa…

FLORA, MARCHESE
E goder voi potrete?

ACT ONE

Prelude [1, 16]

Scene 1

Paris, around the year 1850. A drawing room in Violetta's house. At the back is a door leading to another room; there are two further doors at either side; on the left a fireplace with a mirror above it. In the centre of the room, a richly laid table.

(Violetta, seated on a divan, is talking with the Doctor and some friends, while other guests go to meet a group of new arrivals, among whom are the Baron and Flora, who is escorted by the Marquis.)[2]

GUESTS I
  The invitation was for earlier,
  you've arrived late.

GUESTS II
                  We were playing cards at Flora's,
  the time flew past as we gambled.

VIOLETTA *(going to meet them)*
  Flora, my friends, you will make the remainder
  of the night glitter with new pleasure,
  our party will be more lively when we drink together.

FLORA, MARQUIS
  Do you feel strong enough to enjoy yourself?

VIOLETTA
>Lo voglio;
al piacere m'affido, ed io soglio
con tal farmaco i mali sopir.

**VIOLETTA, FLORA, BARONE, DOTTORE, MARCHESE,
INVITI**
Sì, la vita s'addoppia al gioir.

Scena II

*(Il Visconte Gastone de Létorières entra con Alfredo Germont. Servi
affaccendati intorno alla mensa.)*

GASTONE
In Alfredo Germont, o signora,
ecco un altro che molto v'onora;
pochi amici a lui simili sono.

VIOLETTA *(Dà la mano ad Alfredo, che gliela bacia.)*
Mio Visconte, mercé di tal dono.

MARCHESE
Caro Alfredo…

ALFREDO
>Marchese…

(Si stringono la mano.)

GASTONE *(ad Alfredo)*
>T'ho detto:
l'amistà qui s'intreccia al diletto.

(I servi frattanto avranno imbandito le vivande.)

VIOLETTA *(ai servi)*
Pronto è il tutto?

(Un servo accenna di sì.)

>Miei cari, sedete;
è al convito che s'apre ogni cor.

VIOLETTA
                              I want to;
    I shall trust in pleasure, it is a reliable
    remedy to keep my illness at bay.

VIOLETTA, FLORA, BARON, DOCTOR, MARQUIS,
    GUESTS
    Yes, life is to be enjoyed.

Scene 2

(Viscount Gaston de Létorières enters with Alfredo Germont. Servants busy themselves around the tables.)

GASTON
    Alfredo Germont, Madame,
    is another who esteems you highly;
    few men have proved such good friends.

VIOLETTA *(offering her hand to Alfredo, who kisses it)*
    Thank you for bringing me such a gift, Viscount.

MARQUIS
    My dear Alfredo!

ALFREDO
                              Marquis…

(They shake hands.)

GASTON *(to Alfredo)*
                              As I told you,
    friendship goes hand in hand with pleasure here.

(The servants have meanwhile prepared the tables for supper.)

VIOLETTA *(to the servants)*
    Is everything ready?

(A servant signs that it is.)

                              My dear friends, sit down;
    at table we can open our hearts.

FLORA, ALFREDO, GASTONE, BARONE, DOTTORE,
MARCHESE, INVITI
Ben diceste; le cure segrete
fuga sempre l'amico licor.

(*Siedono in modo che Violetta resti tra Alfredo e Gastone;
di fronte vi sarà Flora, tra il marchese ed il Barone.*)

È al convito che s'apre ogni cor.

GASTONE (*parla piano a Violetta, poi dice*)
Sempre Alfredo a voi pensa.

VIOLETTA

Scherzate?

GASTONE
Egra foste, e ogni dì con affanno
qui volò, di voi chiese.

VIOLETTA

Cessate.
Nulla son io per lui.

GASTONE

Non v'inganno.

VIOLETTA (*ad Alfredo*)
Vero è dunque? Onde è ciò? Nol comprendo.

ALFREDO (*sospirando*)
Sì, egli è ver.

VIOLETTA (*ad Alfredo*)
Le mie grazie vi rendo.
Voi, Barone, non feste altrettanto.

BARONE
Vi conosco da un anno soltanto.

VIOLETTA
Ed ei solo da qualche minuto.

FLORA, ALFREDO, GASTON, BARON, DOCTOR,
  MARQUIS, GUESTS
  Well said, and let good wine
  banish for ever our deepest cares.

(They place themselves so that Violetta is sitting between Alfredo and Gaston. Opposite sit the Marquis and Baron, with Flora between them.)

  At table we can open our hearts.

GASTON *(speaking quietly to Violetta, then saying:)*
  Alfredo thinks of you all the time.

VIOLETTA

                              Are you joking?

GASTON
  When you were ill he anxiously hurried here
  every day to ask after you.

VIOLETTA

                    Stop it,
  I mean nothing to him.

GASTON

                    I am not deceiving you.

VIOLETTA *(to Alfredo)*
  Is this true? How can it be? I don't understand.

ALFREDO *(with a sigh)*
  Yes, it's true.

VIOLETTA *(to Alfredo)*
              Please accept my thanks.
  You never did as much, Baron.

BARON
  I've only known you for a year.

VIOLETTA
  And he's only known me for a few minutes.

(Ride.)

FLORA *(piano al Barone)*
Meglio fora se aveste taciuto.

BARONE *(piano a Flora)*
M'è increscioso quel giovin.

FLORA
                              Perché?
A me invece simpatico egli è.

GASTONE *(ad Alfredo)*
E tu dunque non apri più bocca?

MARCHESE *(a Violetta)*
È a madama che scuoterlo tocca.

VIOLETTA *(mesce ad Alfredo)*
Sarò l'Ebe che versa.

ALFREDO *(con galanteria)*
                              E ch'io bramo
immortal come quella.

TUTTI
                    Beviamo!

GASTONE
O Barone, né un verso, né un viva
troverete in quest'ora giuliva?

(Il Barone accenna di no.)

(ad Alfredo)

Dunque a te!

VIOLETTA, FLORA, DOTTORE, MARCHESE, INVITI
              Sì, sì, un brindisi.

ALFREDO
                        L'estro
non m'arride.

(She laughs.)

FLORA *(quietly, to the Baron)*
 You shouldn't have said that.

BARON *(quietly, to Flora)*
 That young man annoys me.

FLORA
        Why?
 He seems rather nice to me.

GASTON *(to Alfredo)*
 So haven't you anything else to say?

Marquis *(to Violetta)*
 It's up to Madame to make him speak.

VIOLETTA *(pouring wine for Alfredo)*
 I shall be Hebe the cup-bearer.

ALFREDO *(gallantly)*
        And I would wish you
 immortality, like her.

ALL
     Let's drink!

GASTON
 Baron, can't you produce some verse
 or toast at this happy moment?

(The Baron shakes his head.)

(to Alfredo)

 Well, it's up to you!

VIOLETTA, FLORA, DOCTOR, MARQUIS, GUESTS
    Yes, yes, a toast!

ALFREDO
        I don't feel
 at all inspired.

GASTONE
           E non sei tu maestro?

ALFREDO *(a Violetta)*
   Vi fia grato?

VIOLETTA
           Sì.

ALFREDO *(s'alza)*
           Sì?… L'ho già in cor.

MARCHESE
   Dunque attenti…

TUTTI
           Sì, attenti al cantor.

Brindisi

ALFREDO
   Libiamo ne' lieti calici   [3]
   che la bellezza infiora,
   e la fuggevol ora
   s'inebri a voluttà.
   Libiam ne' dolci fremiti
   che suscita l'amore,

(indicando Violetta)

   poiché quell'occhio al core
   onnipotente va.
   Libiamo, amor fra i calici
   più caldi baci avrà.

TUTTI
   Ah! Libiam, amor fra i calici
   più caldi baci avrà.

VIOLETTA *(s'alza)*
   Tra voi saprò dividere
   il tempo mio giocondo;
   tutto è follia nel mondo

GASTON

But you're so good at such things!

ALFREDO *(to Violetta)*
Would you like me to?

VIOLETTA

Yes.

ALFREDO *(rising)*

Yes? It comes from my heart.

MARQUIS
Pay attention…

ALL

Yes, let's hear the singer.

Brindisi

ALFREDO
Let's drink from glasses   [3]
gaily wreathed with beauty's flowers;
let the fleeting hours feel
the intoxication of pleasure.
Let's drink with the sweet emotion
that love causes,

(gesturing towards Violetta)

for those eyes strike powerfully
into our hearts.
Let's drink, wine will give warmth
to our kisses.

ALL
Ah! Let's drink, wine will give warmth
to our kisses.

VIOLETTA *(rising)*
I wish to share with you
my days of happiness;
everything in the world

ciò che non è piacer.
Godiam, fugace e rapido
è il gaudio dell'amore;
è un fior che nasce e muore,
né più si può goder.
Godiam, c'invita un fervido
accento lusinghier.

TUTTI
Ah! Godiamo, la tazza e il cantico
la notte abbella e il riso,
in questo paradiso
ne scopra il nuovo dì.

VIOLETTA *(ad Alfredo)*
La vita è nel tripudio.

ALFREDO *(a Violetta)*
Quando non s'ami ancora.

VIOLETTA *(ad Alfredo)*
Nol dite a chi l'ignora.

ALFREDO *(a Violetta)*
È il mio destin così.

TUTTI
Ah! sì, godiamo, la tazza e il cantico, *ecc.*

Valzer duetto

(S'ode la musica dall'altra sala.)   [4]

TUTTI
Che è ciò?

VIOLETTA
        Non gradireste ora le danze?

TUTTI
Oh, il gentil pensier! Tutti accettiamo.

except for pleasure is vain.
Let's enjoy ourselves, the joys
of love are quick and fleeting;
love's a flower that lives and dies
and then is enjoyed no more.
Let's enjoy ourselves! We are called
by its passionate summons!

ALL
Ah! Let's enjoy ourselves! Let wine, song
and laughter enrich the night,
let the new day find us
still in this paradise.

VIOLETTA *(to Alfredo)*
Life is all pleasure.

ALFREDO *(to Violetta)*
But if one has not yet found love...

VIOLETTA *(to Alfredo)*
Don't tell me... I know nothing of that.

ALFREDO *(to Violetta)*
That is my destiny.

ALL
Ah! Yes, let's enjoy ourselves, *etc.*

Waltz duo

(Music is heard from the next room.) [4]

ALL
What's that?

VIOLETTA
Wouldn't you like to dance now?

ALL
Oh, what a happy thought! We all accept.

VIOLETTA
Usciamo dunque!

(*S'avviano alla porta di mezzo, ma Violetta è colta da subito pallore.*)

Ohimè!

TUTTI
Che avete?

VIOLETTA
Nulla,
nulla.

(*Fa qualche passo.*)

TUTTI
Che mai v'arresta?

VIOLETTA
Usciamo!

(*È obbligata a nuovamente fermarsi e sedere.*)

Oh Dio!

TUTTI
Ancora!

ALFREDO
Voi soffrite.

TUTTI
Oh! ciel! ch'è questo?

VIOLETTA
Un tremito che provo!

(*Indica l'altra sala.*)

Or là passate…
Fra poco anch'io sarò.

TUTTI
Come bramate.

(*Tutti passano all'altra sala, meno Alfredo.*)

VIOLETTA
Let's go next door!

(They move towards the centre door, but Violetta suddenly turns pale.)

Oh!

ALL
What's the matter?

VIOLETTA
It's nothing,
nothing.

(She takes a few steps.)

ALL
What's troubling you?

VIOLETTA
Let's go!

(She has to pause again, and sits down.)

O Heavens!

ALL
Again!

ALFREDO
You're unwell.

ALL
O Heavens, what's the matter?

VIOLETTA
I feel a trembling!

(She points to the next room.)

But go in...
I'll join you in a moment.

ALL
As you wish.

(They all go into the other room, apart from Alfredo.)

Scena III

VIOLETTA *(Si alza e va a guardarsi allo specchio.)*
  Oh, qual pallor!

(Si volge e s'accorge d'Alfredo.)

                    Voi qui!

ALFREDO

                    Cessata è l'ansia

  che vi turbò?

VIOLETTA

              Sto meglio.

ALFREDO

                      Ah, in cotal guisa

  v'ucciderete. Aver v'è d'uopo cura
  dell'esser vostro.

VIOLETTA

            E lo potrei?

ALFREDO

                        Oh! se mia

  foste, custode veglierei pe' vostri
  soavi dì.

VIOLETTA

          Che dite? Ha forse alcuno
  cura di me?

ALFREDO *(con fuoco)*

          Perché nessuno al mondo
  v'ama...

VIOLETTA

        Nessun?

ALFREDO

              ...tranne sol io...

Scene 3

VIOLETTA *(rising, and looking in the mirror)*
　Oh, how pale I am!

(She turns round and notices Alfredo.)

　　　　　　You're still here!

ALFREDO
　　　　　　　　　Has that moment
　of discomfort passed?

VIOLETTA
　　　　　I feel better.

ALFREDO
　　　　　　　　　Ah, if you go on like this
　you'll kill yourself. You should take better care
　of yourself.

VIOLETTA
　　　　　And how can I do that?

ALFREDO
　　　　　　　　　Ah! If you were mine,
　I would watch over
　your tender life.

VIOLETTA
　　　　　What are you saying? Does anyone ever
　look after me?

ALFREDO *(ardently)*
　　　　　　That's because nobody in the world
　loves you…

VIOLETTA
　　　　　Nobody?

ALFREDO
　　　　　　…apart from me.

91

VIOLETTA

Gli è vero!
Sì grande amor dimenticato avea.

(ridendo)

ALFREDO
Ridete! E in voi v'ha un core?

VIOLETTA
Un cor? Sì, forse. E a che lo richiedete?

ALFREDO
Ah, se ciò fosse, non potreste allora
celiar.

VIOLETTA
Dite davvero?

ALFREDO
Io non v'inganno.

VIOLETTA
Da molto è che mi amate?

ALFREDO
Ah sì, da un anno.

Un dì felice, eterea,   [5]
mi balenaste innante,
e da quel dì tremante
vissi d'ignoto amor.
Di quell'amor ch'è palpito   [6]
dell'universo intero,
misterioso, altero,
croce e delizia al cor.

VIOLETTA
Ah, se ciò è ver, fuggitemi.   [7]
Solo amistade io v'offro;
amar non so, né soffro
un così eroico amore.

VIOLETTA

That's true!
I'd forgotten your grand passion.

(laughing)

ALFREDO
You laugh! Have you no heart?

VIOLETTA
A heart? Yes, perhaps. But why do you ask?

ALFREDO
Ah, because if you had, you wouldn't
laugh at me.

VIOLETTA

Do you really mean that?

ALFREDO

I'm not lying to you.

VIOLETTA
Have you loved me for long?

ALFREDO

Yes, for a year.

One blessed day you appeared   [5]
before me like a vision,
and from that day I have lived
in the turmoil of my unspoken love:
a love that beats   [6]
like the pulse of the whole world,
mysterious, unattainable,
the torment and joy of my heart.

VIOLETTA
Ah, if that is so, you must leave me.   [7]
I can offer you only friendship;
I cannot love, I could never bear
such a heroic love.

Io sono franca, ingenua;
altra cercar dovete;
non arduo troverete
dimenticarmi allor.

ALFREDO
Oh amore
misterioso, altero,
croce e delizia al cor.

VIOLETTA
Non arduo troverete
dimenticarmi allor.

GASTONE *(sulla porta di mezzo)*
Ebben?... che diavol fate?

VIOLETTA
Si folleggiava.

GASTONE
Ah! ah! Sta ben! restate!

(Rientra.)

VIOLETTA *(ad Alfredo)*
Amor dunque non più. Vi garba il patto?

ALFREDO
Io v'obbedisco. Parto.

(per andarsene)

VIOLETTA
A tal giungeste?

(Si toglie un fiore dal seno.)

Prendete questo fiore.

ALFREDO
Perché?

I'm being honest and plain;
you must find someone else;
then you will not find it so difficult
to forget me.

ALFREDO
O love,
mysterious, unattainable,
the torment and joy of my heart.

VIOLETTA
You will not find it so difficult
to forget me.

GASTON *(in the central doorway)*
Well? What the devil are you doing here?

VIOLETTA
We're just being silly.

GASTON
Ha, ha! Very well, carry on!

(He goes back.)

VIOLETTA *(to Alfredo)*
So no more about love. Agreed?

ALFREDO
I shall do as you say. I shall leave you.

(about to go)

VIOLETTA
Just like that?

(She takes a flower from her breast.)

Take this flower.

ALFREDO
Why?

VIOLETTA
     Per riportarlo.

ALFREDO *(tornando)*
           Quando?

VIOLETTA
               Quando
sarà appassito.

ALFREDO
       Oh ciel! Domani?

VIOLETTA
                 Ebbene,
domani.

ALFREDO *(Prende con trasporto il fiore.)*
     Io son felice!

VIOLETTA
    D'amarmi dite ancora?

ALFREDO *(per partire)*
           Oh, quanto v'amo!
   Io son felice.

VIOLETTA
   D'amarmi dite ancora?
   Partite?

ALFREDO *(tornando a lei e baciandole la mano)*
     Parto.

VIOLETTA
      Addio.

ALFREDO
   Di più non bramo.

VIOLETTA
So that you can bring it back.

ALFREDO *(turning back)*
                                When?

VIOLETTA
                                        When
it has withered.

ALFREDO
                O Heavens! Tomorrow?

VIOLETTA
                                        Very well then,
tomorrow.

ALFREDO *(rapturously taking the flower)*
                I am so happy.

VIOLETTA
You won't tell me again that you love me?

ALFREDO *(about to go)*
                                        Oh! How I love you,
I'm so happy

VIOLETTA
You won't tell me again that you love me?
Are you going now?

ALFREDO *(going back to her and kissing her hand)*
                I'm going.

VIOLETTA
                        Goodbye, then.

ALFREDO
I ask for nothing more.

VIOLETTA, ALFREDO
                Addio.

(Esce Alfredo.)

Scena IV

(Tutti gli altri tornano dalla sala riscaldati dalle danze.)

Stretta

FLORA, GASTONE, BARONE, DOTTORE, MARCHESE,
   INVITI
   Si ridesta in ciel l'aurora,   [8]
   e n'è forza di partire;
   mercé a voi, gentil signora,
   di sì splendido gioir.
   La città di feste è piena,
   volge il tempo dei piacer;
   nel riposo ancor la lena
   si ritempri per goder.

(Partono dalla destra.)

Scena V

VIOLETTA *(sola)*
   È strano!... è strano!... In core
   scolpiti ho quegli accenti!
   Saria per me sventura un serio amore?
   Che risolvi, o turbata anima mia?
   Null'uomo ancora t'accendeva... Oh, gioia
   ch'io non conobbi esser amata amando!
   E sdegnarla poss'io
   per l'aride follie del viver mio?

   Ah, fors'è lui che l'anima   [9]
   solinga ne' tumulti
   godea sovente pingere
   de' suoi colori occulti!...
   Lui, che modesto e vigile
   all'egre soglie ascese,

VIOLETTA, ALFREDO
                    Goodbye.

(Alfredo leaves.)

Scene 4

(The other guests, flushed from dancing, return from the next room.)

Stretta

FLORA, GASTON, BARON, DOCTOR, MARQUIS,
    GUESTS
    Dawn is beginning to lighten the sky: [8]
    we must take our leave now;
    thank you, dear Madame,
    for such wonderful entertainment.
    The city sparkles with feasting,
    time goes by in a whirl of enjoyment;
    we shall rest and refresh ourselves
    for further rounds of pleasure.

(They leave from the door on the right.)

Scene 5

VIOLETTA *(alone)*
    How strange! How strange!
    That voice has struck deep into my heart!
    Would true love be so terrible?
    What do you think, my troubled spirit?
    No man has ever inspired you... Oh, I have never known
    the joy of loving and being loved!
    And could I reject him
    for my life of empty pleasure?

    Ah, perhaps he is the one that my heart,   [9]
    lonely even among crowds,
    would often delight in imagining
    in mysterious colours.
    He, who modestly and attentively
    came to me when I was ill,

e nuova febbre accese,
destandomi all'amor.
A quell'amor ch'è palpito
dell'universo intero,
misterioso, altero,
croce e delizia al cor.

A me, fanciulla, un candido
e trepido desire
quest'effigiò dolcissimo
signor dell'avvenire
quando ne' cieli il raggio
di sua beltà vedea,
e tutta me pascea
di quel divino error.
Sentia che amore è palpito
dell'universo intero,
misterioso, altero,
croce e delizia al cor.

(Resta concentrata un istante; poi, scuotendosi:)

Follie!… follie!… delirio vano è questo!…
Povera donna, sola,
abbandonata in questo
popoloso deserto
che appellano Parigi,
che spero or più? Che far degg'io? Gioire!
Di voluttà ne' vortici perire!
Gioir!

Sempre libera degg'io   [10]
folleggiar di gioia in gioia,
vo' che scorra il viver mio
pei sentieri del piacer.
Nasca il giorno, o il giorno muoia,
sempre lieta ne' ritrovi,
a diletti sempre nuovi
dee volare il mio pensier.

and brought on a new fever
by awakening love in me!
The love that beats
like the pulse of the whole world;
mysterious, unattainable,
the torment and joy of my heart.

When I was a girl, it sweetly
appeared in my longings
as a pure and timid image
of the future man in my life;
when I imagined the glow
of his beauty in the heavens
I would live entirely
in that divine illusion.
I knew that it was love that beats
like the pulse of the whole world,
mysterious, unattainable,
the torment and joy of my heart.

(She remains lost in thought for a moment, then comes to herself.)

It's madness! It's just a silly fantasy!
I'm a poor woman,
lonely and abandoned
in this teeming desert
they call Paris;
what have I to hope for? What can I do? Live for pleasure!
Drown in the whirlpool of the senses!
Live for pleasure!

I must be entirely free   [10]
to flutter from one joy to another,
I want my life to continue
along the paths of pleasure.
As each day comes, as each day goes,
I shall always gaily turn
to new delights
to make my spirits soar.

ALFREDO *(sotto al balcone)*
    Amor è palpito [6]
    dell'universo intero,
    misterioso, altero,
    croce e delizia al cor.

VIOLETTA
    Oh!… Amore!… Follie!…
    Gioir!
    Sempre libera degg'io, *ecc.*
    dee volare il mio pensier.

ALFREDO *(sotto al balcone)*
    Amor è palpito
    dell'universo…

(Violetta esce a sinistra.)

ALFREDO *(beneath the balcony)*
    The love that beats   [6]
    like the pulse of the whole world,
    mysterious, unattainable,
    the torment and joy of my heart.

VIOLETTA
    Oh!... Love!... Madness!...
    Pleasure!
    I must be entirely free, *etc.*
    to make my spirits soar.

ALFREDO *(beneath the balcony)*
    The love that beats
    like the pulse of the whole world...

(Violetta leaves by the door on the left.)

ATTO SECONDO

Scena I

Casa di campagna presso Parigi. Salotto terreno. Nel fondo in faccia agli spettatori è un camino, sopra il quale uno specchio ed un orologio; fra due porte chiuse da cristalli che mettono ad un giardino. Al primo piano due altre porte, una di fronte all'altra. Sedie, tavolini, qualche libro, l'occorrente per iscrivere.

(Alfredo entra in costume da caccia.)

ALFREDO *(deponendo il fucile)*
  Lunge da lei per me non v'ha diletto!
  Volaron già tre lune
  dacché la mia Violetta
  agi per me lasciò, dovizie, amori
  e le pompose feste,
  ov'agli omaggi avvezza
  vedea schiavo ciascun di sua bellezza…
  Ed or contenta in questi ameni luoghi
  tutto scorda per me. Qui presso a lei
  io rinascer mi sento,
  e dal soffio d'amor rigenerato
  scordo ne' gaudi suoi tutto il passato.

  De' miei bollenti spiriti   [11]
  il giovanile ardore
  ella temprò col placido
  sorriso dell'amor!
  Dal dì che disse: vivere
  io voglio a te fedel,

ACT TWO

Scene 1

A house in the country near Paris. A drawing room on the ground floor. At the back, facing the audience, is a fireplace with a mirror and a clock above it. On either side of the fireplace are French windows which lead into the garden. In the foreground are two other doors facing one another. There are chairs, tables, a few books and writing implements.

(Alfredo enters in hunting costume.)

ALFREDO *(putting down his gun)*
    Life holds no pleasure for me when she is away!
    It is three months now
    since for my sake Violetta
    abandoned her life of love and luxury,
    and the glittering parties
    where she basked in the homage
    of all those who were slaves to her beauty.
    For my sake she abandoned it all
    and now lives happily in this charming house.
    Here in her company I feel reborn
    and, revived by the breath of love, I can forget
    the past and delight in the joys she offers me.

    The youthful ardour   [11]
    of my passionate nature
    has been soothed by her
    gentle, loving smile.
    From the day when she said
    'I want to live faithfully with you',

dell'universo immemore
io vivo quasi in ciel.

Scena II

(Annina entra affannosa in arnese da viaggio.)

ALFREDO
Annina, donde vieni?

ANNINA
                    Da Parigi.

ALFREDO
Chi tel commise?

ANNINA
                    Fu la mia signora.

ALFREDO
Perché?

ANNINA
            Per alienar cavalli, cocchi
e quanto ancor possiede.

ALFREDO
                        Che mai sento!

ANNINA
Lo spendio è grande a viver qui solinghi…

ALFREDO
E tacevi?

ANNINA
            Mi fu il silenzio imposto.

ALFREDO
Imposto!… Or v'abbisogna?…

ANNINA
                        Mille luigi.

I have been oblivious to the world
and live now as though in paradise.

Scene 2

(Annina, dressed for travelling, enters in agitation.)

ALFREDO
Annina, where have you been?

ANNINA
                    To Paris.

ALFREDO
Who sent you there?

ANNINA
                    My mistress.

ALFREDO
Why?

ANNINA
        To sell the horses, the coaches
and all the rest of her possessions.

ALFREDO
                        Whatever do you mean?

ANNINA
Living here alone is very expensive...

ALFREDO
And you said nothing?

ANNINA
                    I was told to keep quiet.

ALFREDO
You were told? So how much do you need?

ANNINA
                            A thousand louis.

ALFREDO
Or vanne… andrò a Parigi.
Questo colloquio non sappia la signora;
il tutto valgo a riparare ancora.

(Annina parte.)

Scena III

ALFREDO *(solo)*
Oh mio rimorso! Oh infamia!
Io vissi in tale errore!
Ma il turpe sogno a frangere
il ver mi balenò!
Per poco in seno acquetati,
o grido dell'onore;
m'avrai securo vindice;
quest'onta laverò.
Oh mio rossor! Oh infamia!
Ah sì, quest'onta laverò.

(Esce.)

Scena IV

(Violetta entra con alcune carte, parlando con Annina; dietro loro Giuseppe.)

VIOLETTA
Alfredo?

ANNINA
Per Parigi or or partiva.

VIOLETTA
E tornerà?

ANNINA
Pria che tramonti il giorno…
Dirvel m'impose…

VIOLETTA
È strano!

ALFREDO
You may go… I'll go to Paris myself.
Don't tell Madame that we've spoken;
there's still time to save the situation.

(Annina leaves.)

Scene 3

ALFREDO *(alone)*
Oh, what remorse! How shameful!
I've been living in such error!
But the truth has come in a flash
to shatter my ignoble dreams!
O voice of honour, be still in my heart
for a little while longer;
you shall certainly be avenged,
I shall wash away this disgrace.
Oh, what dishonour, how shameful!
Ah, I shall wash away this disgrace.

(Alfredo leaves.)

Scene 4

(Violetta comes in with some papers, speaking with Annina. Giuseppe follows them.)

VIOLETTA
Where's Alfredo?

ANNINA
He's just left for Paris.

VIOLETTA
When will he be back?

ANNINA
Before it gets dark.
He asked me to tell you.

VIOLETTA
How strange!

GIUSEPPE *(presentandole una lettera)*
Per voi.

VIOLETTA *(La prende.)*
   Sta ben. In breve
giungerà un uom d'affari. Entri all'istante.

(Annina e Giuseppe partono.)

Scena V

(Violetta, sola, apre la lettera.)

VIOLETTA *(leggendo)*
Ah, ah! Scopriva Flora il mio ritiro,
e m'invita a danzar per questa sera!

(Getta il foglio sul tavolino e siede.)

Invan m'aspetterà.

GIUSEPPE *(entrando)*
     È qui un signore.

VIOLETTA
Ah! Sarà lui che attendo.

(Accenna a Giuseppe d'introdurlo. Egli avanza due sedie e parte.)

GERMONT
Madamigella Valery?

VIOLETTA
    Son io.

GERMONT
D'Alfredo il padre in me vedete.

VIOLETTA *(Sorpresa, l'invita a sedersi.)*
      Voi?

GERMONT *(sedendo)*
Sì, dell'incauto, che a ruina corre,
ammaliato da voi.

GIUSEPPE *(giving her a letter)*
This is for you.

VIOLETTA *(taking it)*
Very well. A gentleman will shortly
be coming on business. Show him in immediately.

(Annina and Giuseppe go out.)

Scene 5

(Violetta, alone, opens the letter.)

VIOLETTA *(reading)*
Ha, ha! Flora has found out my hiding place
and invites me to a dance this evening!

(She throws the letter onto a table and sits down.)

She will expect me in vain.

GIUSEPPE *(entering)*
A gentleman has arrived.

VIOLETTA
He must be the man I'm expecting.

(She gestures to Giuseppe to show him in. He draws two chairs and leaves.)

GERMONT
Mademoiselle Valéry?

VIOLETTA
Yes.

GERMONT
I am the father of Alfredo.

VIOLETTA *(Surprised, she invites him to sit down.)*
Are you indeed?

GERMONT *(sitting down)*
Yes, of the rash boy who is heading for ruin,
because you have led him astray.

VIOLETTA *(alzandosi, risentita)*
    Donna son io, signore, ed in mia casa;
    ch'io vi lasci assentite,
    più per voi, che per me.

(per uscire)

GERMONT
                (Quai modi!) Pure…

VIOLETTA
    Tratto in error voi foste!

(Torna a sedere.)

GERMONT
              De' suoi beni
    dono vuol farvi.

VIOLETTA
           Non l'osò finora…
    Rifiuterei.

GERMONT *(guardando intorno)*
        Pur tanto lusso…

VIOLETTA *(Gli dà una carta.)*
                  A tutti
    è mistero quest'atto… A voi nol sia.

GERMONT *(Scorre le carte.)*
    Ciel! Che discopro! D'ogni vostro avere
    or volete spogliarvi?
    Ah, il passato, perché, perché v'accusa!

VIOLETTA *(con entusiasmo)*
    Più non esiste. Or amo Alfredo, e Dio
    lo cancellò col pentimento mio!

GERMONT
    Nobili sensi invero!

VIOLETTA *(rising in indignation)*
I am a lady, sir, and this is my own house;
allow me to leave you,
rather for your sake than for mine.

(She is about to leave.)

GERMONT
(What manners!) And yet…

VIOLETTA
You are mistaken!

(sitting down again)

GERMONT
He intends to make over to you everything
he possesses.

VIOLETTA
He has never dared to do anything of the sort…
I would refuse.

GERMONT *(looking around)*
Yet you live in luxury…

VIOLETTA *(handing him a document)*
This document
must be a secret to everybody except to you.

GERMONT *(looking through the papers)*
Heavens, what a discovery! Do you really intend
to get rid of all your possessions?
Ah, your past is reproaching you!

VIOLETTA *(with spirit)*
It no longer exists. I love Alfredo now, and God
has wiped clean the past with my repentance!

GERMONT
Noble sentiments, indeed!

113

VIOLETTA

            Oh, come dolce
mi suona il vostro accento!

GERMONT *(alzandosi)*

               Ed a tai sensi
un sacrifizio chieggo.

VIOLETTA

             Ah, no, tacete!…
Terribil cosa chiedereste certo…
Il previdi… v'attesi… era felice
troppo!

GERMONT

     D'Alfredo il padre
la sorte, l'avvenir domanda or qui
de' suoi due figli!

VIOLETTA

       Di due figli!

GERMONT

               Sì.

Pura siccome un angelo   [12]
Iddio mi die' una figlia;
se Alfredo nega riedere
in seno alla famiglia,
l'amato e amante giovine,
cui sposa andar dovea,
or si ricusa al vincolo
che lieti ne rendeva…
Deh, non mutate in triboli
le rose dell'amor.
A' prieghi miei resistere
non voglia il vostro cor.

VIOLETTA

Ah, comprendo… Dovrò per alcun tempo
da Alfredo allontanarmi… Doloroso
fora per me… pur…

VIOLETTA

Oh, how kindly
you speak now!

GERMONT *(rising)*

And on account of those sentiments
I must ask you to make a sacrifice.

VIOLETTA

Ah, no! Be silent!
You will ask something dreadful of me!
I foresaw this... I was expecting you... My happiness
was too great!

GERMONT

The father of Alfredo
now pleads with you for the future
of both his children!

VIOLETTA

Both children?

GERMONT

Yes.

God granted me a daughter   [12]
who is as pure as an angel;
but if Alfredo refuses to return
to the bosom of his family,
the young man she loves, and who loves her,
the man whom she is to marry,
will withdraw from the union
that would make them so happy.
Come, do not allow the roses of love
to turn to thorns.
No, I cannot believe that your heart
will be unmoved by my pleas.

VIOLETTA

Ah, I understand. For a while
I must separate from Alfredo... It will be painful
for me... but...

GERMONT

Non è ciò che chiedo.

VIOLETTA

Cielo! Che più cercate?... Offersi assai!

GERMONT

Pur non basta...

VIOLETTA

Volete che per sempre
a lui rinunzi?

GERMONT

È d'uopo!...

VIOLETTA

Ah no... giammai!
No, mai!

Non sapete quale affetto   [13]
vivo, immenso m'arda in petto?
Che né amici né parenti
io non conto tra' viventi?
e che Alfredo m'ha giurato
che in lui tutto troverò?
Non sapete che colpita
d'atro morbo è la mia vita?
che già presso il fin ne vedo?
Ch'io mi separi da Alfredo?
Ah, il supplizio è sì spietato
che a morir preferirò.

GERMONT

È grave il sacrifizio;
ma pur, tranquilla uditemi...
Bella voi siete e giovine...
Col tempo...

GERMONT

That is not what I am asking of you.

VIOLETTA

Heavens, what more could you ask? I have offered so much!

GERMONT

And yet it is not enough.

VIOLETTA

Do you wish me
to give him up for ever?

GERMONT

It is necessary.

VIOLETTA

Ah, no! Never!
No, never!

Don't you realize what a vital,   [13]
immense love burns in my heart?
That I have no friends or family
still living in the world?
Or that Alfredo swore to me
that I should find them all in him?
Don't you know that my life
is threatened by a cruel illness?
And that my end is near?
Part from Alfredo!
Ah, it would be so cruel a torment
that I would rather die.

GERMONT

It is a great sacrifice;
but listen to me patiently.
You are young, and you are beautiful.
In time…

VIOLETTA

Ah, più nol dite...
V'intendo... M'è impossibile...
Lui solo amar vogl'io!

GERMONT

Sia pure... ma volubile
sovente è l'uom...

VIOLETTA *(colpita)*

Gran Dio!

GERMONT

Un dì, quando le veneri
il tempo avrà fugate,
fia presto il tedio a sorgere...
Che sarà allor?... Pensate...
per voi non avran balsamo
i più soavi affetti,
poiché dal ciel non furono
tai nodi benedetti.

VIOLETTA

È vero!

GERMONT

Ah, dunque sperdasi
tal sogno seduttore...

VIOLETTA

È vero! è ver!

GERMONT

Siate di mia famiglia
l'angiol consolatore...
Violetta, deh pensateci,
ne siete in tempo ancor.
È Dio che ispira, o giovine,
tai detti a un genitor.

VIOLETTA
> Ah, say no more...
> I understand what you mean. I could never do that...
> I wish to love him alone!

GERMONT
> That may be so, but men
> are often fickle.

VIOLETTA *(shocked)*
> Dear God!

GERMONT
> One day, when time
> has withered your charms,
> boredom will make its appearance.
> What will happen then? Just think,
> even the tenderest affection
> will be of no comfort,
> for your union
> has not been blessed by Heaven.

VIOLETTA
> How true!

GERMONT
> Ah, so abandon
> this seductive illusion!

VIOLETTA
> How true!

GERMONT
> Be a consoling angel
> for my family! Come now,
> Violetta, consider it,
> there is still time for you.
> Young lady, God himself is inspiring
> a parent to speak in this way.

VIOLETTA *(con estremo dolore)*
   (Così alla misera, ch'è un dì caduta,
   di più risorgere speranza è muta!
   Se pur benefico le indulga Iddio,
   l'uomo implacabile per lei sarà.)

GERMONT
   Siate di mia famiglia
   l'angiol consolator.

VIOLETTA *(a Germont piangendo)*
   Ah! Dite alla giovine sì bella e pura,   [14]
   ch'avvi una vittima della sventura,
   cui resta un unico raggio di bene...
   che a lei il sacrifica e che morrà!

GERMONT
   Piangi, o misera!... Supremo, il veggo,
   è il sacrifizio ch'ora ti chieggo...
   Sento nell'anima già le tue pene;
   coraggio, e il nobil tuo cor vincerà!

VIOLETTA
   Dite alla giovine sì bella e pura, *ecc.*

GERMONT
   Ah, supremo, il veggo, *ecc.*
   Piangi, piangi, o misera.
   Coraggio, e il nobil tuo cor vincerà!

VIOLETTA
   Imponete.

GERMONT
           Non amarlo ditegli.

VIOLETTA
   Nol crederà.

GERMONT
           Partite.

VIOLETTA *(with deep sorrow)*
    (So a wretched woman who has once fallen
    can never hope to rise again!
    Even if God shows her mercy,
    mankind will never forgive.)

GERMONT
    Be a consoling angel
    for my family.

VIOLETTA *(to Germont, weeping)*
    Ah! Tell your daughter, so fair and pure,   [14]
    that there is a victim of misfortune
    who for her sake has sacrificed her only
    remaining ray of happiness, and soon will die.

GERMONT
    Weep, poor girl, weep! I understand
    what a supreme sacrifice I am asking of you…
    Your pain strikes me to the heart;
    be brave, your noble heart will triumph!

VIOLETTA
    Tell your daughter, *etc.*

GERMONT
    I understand what a supreme sacrifice, *etc.*
    Weep, poor girl, weep!
    Be brave, your noble heart will triumph!

VIOLETTA
    Tell me what to do.

GERMONT
                  Say you no longer love him.

VIOLETTA
    He won't believe me.

GERMONT
                Leave him, then.

VIOLETTA

Seguirammi.

GERMONT
Allor...

VIOLETTA
Qual figlia m'abbracciate, forte
così sarò.

(S'abbracciano.)

Tra breve ei vi fia reso,
ma afflitto oltre ogni dire. A suo conforto
di colà volerete.

(Indicandogli il giardino, va per scrivere.)

GERMONT
Che pensate?

VIOLETTA
Sapendol, v'opporreste al pensier mio.

GERMONT
Generosa!... E per voi che far poss'io?
Che far poss'io, o generosa?

VIOLETTA *(tornando a lui)*
Morrò!... La mia memoria
non fia ch'ei maledica,
se le mie pene orribili
vi sia chi almen gli dica.

GERMONT
No, generosa, vivere,
e lieta, voi dovrete,
mercé di queste lagrime
dal cielo un giorno avrete.

VIOLETTA
Conosca il sacrifizio
ch'io consumai d'amore...

VIOLETTA

He'll follow me.

GERMONT
Then…

VIOLETTA
Embrace me as though I were your daughter:
it will give me strength.

(They embrace.)

He will soon be restored to you,
but more wretched than words can tell. You must
wait there to console him.

(She points to the garden, then goes to write something.)

GERMONT
What are you doing?

VIOLETTA
You would only oppose me if you knew.

GERMONT
Generous heart! And what can I do for you?
How can I repay your generosity?

VIOLETTA *(turning to him)*
I am going to die! I don't want him
to curse my memory,
I would like someone to tell him
how much I have suffered.

GERMONT
No, generous heart,
you must live and be happy.
One day Heaven will reward you
for these tears.

VIOLETTA
He must learn of the sacrifice
I have made of that love

che sarà suo fin l'ultimo
sospiro del mio cor.

GERMONT
Premiato il sacrifizio
sarà del vostro core,
d'un'opra così nobile
sarete fiera allor.

VIOLETTA
Conosca il sacrifizio, *ecc.*

GERMONT
Premiato il sacrifizio, *ecc.*

VIOLETTA
Qui giunge alcun: partite.

GERMONT
Oh, grato v'è il cor mio!

VIOLETTA
                                Partite.
Non ci vedrem più forse...

(S'abbracciano.)

VIOLETTA e GERMONT
Siate felice... Addio!

(Si allontanano verso la porta.)

VIOLETTA *(piangendo)*
Conosca il sacrifizio
ch'io consumai d'amore...

GERMONT *(È sulla porta.)*
Sì, sì.

VIOLETTA
...che sarà suo fin l'ultimo...

(Il pianto le tronca la parola.)

which will be his alone
until my dying breath.

GERMONT
The sacrifice you have made
of your love will be rewarded;
one day you will be proud
of so noble a gesture.

VIOLETTA
He must learn of the sacrifice, *etc.*

GERMONT
The sacrifice you have made, *etc.*

VIOLETTA
Someone is coming, you must leave now.

GERMONT
Oh, how grateful I am to you!

VIOLETTA
                          Please leave.
We may never meet again…

(They embrace.)

VIOLETTA and GERMONT
May you be happy! Farewell!

(They move towards the door.)

VIOLETTA *(weeping)*
He must learn of the sacrifice
I have made of that love…

GERMONT *(at the door)*
Yes, yes.

VIOLETTA
…which will be his alone…

(She cannot speak for weeping.)

125

Addio!

GERMONT
   Addio!

VIOLETTA e GERMONT
         Felice siate… Addio!

(Germont esce per la porta del giardino.)

Scena VI

VIOLETTA
   Dammi tu forza, o cielo!

(Siede e scrive, poi suona il campanello.)

ANNINA
   Mi richiedeste?

VIOLETTA
            Sì, reca tu stessa
   questo foglio…

ANNINA *(Ne guarda il destinatario e se ne mostra sorpresa.)*
            Oh!

VIOLETTA
            Silenzio… Va' all'istante.

(Annina parte)

   Ed or si scriva a lui…   [15]
   Che gli dirò? Chi men darà il coraggio?

(Piangendo scrive, poi suggella.)

ALFREDO *(entrando)*
   Che fai?

VIOLETTA *(nascondendo la lettera)*
         Nulla.

ALFREDO
            Scrivevi?

Farewell!

GERMONT
          Farewell!

VIOLETTA and GERMONT
                    May you be happy! Farewell!

(Germont leaves by the garden door.)

Scene 6

VIOLETTA
God give me strength!

(She sits down and writes something, then rings the bell.)

ANNINA
You called me?

VIOLETTA
                    Yes, deliver this letter
yourself…

ANNINA *(surprised when she sees who it is addressed to.)*
          Oh!

VIOLETTA
                    Be quiet! Go immediately.

(Annina leaves)

Now I must write to him.   [15]
What can I say? How shall I find the courage to say it?

(Weeping, she writes, then seals what she has written.)

ALFREDO *(entering)*
What are you doing?

VIOLETTA *(hiding the letter)*
                    Nothing.

ALFREDO
                         You're writing something?

VIOLETTA (*confusa*)
Sì... no...

ALFREDO
Qual turbamento!... A chi scrivevi?

VIOLETTA
A te.

ALFREDO
Dammi quel foglio.

VIOLETTA
No, per ora.

ALFREDO
Mi perdona... son io preoccupato.

VIOLETTA (*alzandosi*)
Che fu?

ALFREDO
Giunse mio padre...

VIOLETTA
Lo vedesti?

ALFREDO
Ah, no; severo scritto mi lasciava...
Però l'attendo, t'amerà in vederti.

VIOLETTA (*molto agitata*)
Ch'ei qui non mi sorprenda...
Lascia che m'allontani... tu lo calma...

(*mal frenando il pianto*)

Ai piedi suoi mi getterò... divisi
ei più non ne vorrà. Sarem felici...
perché tu m'ami, Alfredo, non è vero?

ALFREDO
Oh, quanto... Perché piangi?

VIOLETTA *(embarrassed)*
Yes… no…

ALFREDO
You are so upset! Who were you writing to?

VIOLETTA
To you.

ALFREDO
Give me that letter.

VIOLETTA
No, not now.

ALFREDO
Forgive me… I'm worried.

VIOLETTA *(rising)*
What is it?

ALFREDO
My father has arrived…

VIOLETTA
Have you seen him?

ALFREDO
Ah, no; but he left me a stern letter!
I shall wait for him. When he meets you, he will love you.

VIOLETTA *(greatly agitated)*
Don't let him find me here…
Let me go away… You can calm him…

(barely able to suppress her tears)

I'll cast myself down at his feet…
he won't want to separate us then. We'll be happy –
because you love me, Alfredo, don't you?

ALFREDO
Oh, so much! But why are you crying?

VIOLETTA
Di lagrime avea d'uopo... or son tranquilla...

(sforzandosi)

Lo vedi?... ti sorrido...
Lo vedi?... or son tranquilla... ti sorrido.
Sarò là, tra quei fior, presso a te sempre.
Amami, Alfredo, amami quant'io t'amo... Addio!   [16]

(Corre in giardino.)

Scena VII

ALFREDO
Ah, vive sol quel core all'amor mio!

(Siede, prende a caso un libro, quindi si alza, guarda l'ora sull'orologio sovrapposto al camino.)

È tardi ed oggi forse
più non verrà mio padre.

GIUSEPPE *(entrando frettoloso)*
La signora è partita...
l'attendeva un calesse, e sulla via
già corre di Parigi... Annina pure
prima di lei spariva.

ALFREDO
                    Il so, ti calma.

GIUSEPPE
(Che vuol dir ciò?)

(Parte.)

ALFREDO
                    Va forse d'ogni avere
ad affrettar la perdita... Ma Annina
la impedirà.

(Si vede il padre attraversare da lontano il giardino.)

VIOLETTA
I needed to cry, but I'm calm now.

(making an effort)

You see? I'm smiling at you...
You see? I'm calm now... I'm smiling at you.
I shall be there, among the flowers, always close to you.
Love me, Alfredo, love me as much as I love you! Farewell!   [16]

(She runs into the garden.)

Scene 7

ALFREDO
Ah, she lives entirely for my love!

(He sits down, casually picks up a book, reads for a moment, then rises and looks at the clock above the fireplace.)

It's getting late; perhaps my father
won't come today.

GIUSEPPE *(entering hastily)*
Madame has gone away...
a carriage was waiting for her,
and it's now on its way to Paris.
Annina, too, left ahead of her.

ALFREDO
                            I know, don't worry.

GIUSEPPE
(What's all this?)

(He leaves.)

ALFREDO
                    She's probably gone to hasten
the sale of all her things. But Annina
will prevent her.

(In the distance he sees his father crossing the garden.)

Qualcuno è nel giardino?
Chi è là?

(per uscire)

COMMISSIONARIO *(alla porta)*
Il signor Germont?

ALFREDO

Son io.

COMMISSIONARIO

Una dama
da un cocchio, per voi, di qua non lunge,
mi diede questo scritto…

(Dà una lettera ad Alfredo, ne riceve una moneta e parte.)

Scena VIII

ALFREDO
Di Violetta! Perché son io commosso?…
A raggiungerla forse ella m'invita…
Io tremo!… O ciel!… Coraggio!…

(Apre la lettera e legge.)

'Alfredo, al giungervi di questo foglio…'

(gridando, come fulminato)

Ah!

(Volgendosi, si trova a fronte del padre, nelle cui braccia si abbandona, esclamando)

Padre mio!

GERMONT

Mio figlio!
Oh, quanto soffri!… tergi, ah, tergi il pianto…
ritorna di tuo padre orgoglio e vanto.

(Alfredo disperato siede presso il tavolino col volto fra le mani.)

There's somebody in the garden.

Who's there?

(He is about to go out.)

MESSENGER *(at the door)*
Monsieur Germont?

ALFREDO

Yes.

MESSENGER

A lady,

in a carriage, not far from here,
gave me this letter for you.

(He gives Alfredo a letter, accepts a coin and leaves.)

Scene 8

ALFREDO
From Violetta! Why do I feel so disturbed?
Perhaps she's suggesting that I join her?
I'm shaking! Heavens, be brave!

(He opens the letter and reads.)

'Alfredo, by the time you receive this letter...'

(He cries as though struck.)

Ah!

(Turning round, he sees his father standing before him. He throws himself into his arms, crying out:)

Father!

GERMONT
My son!
Oh, how you suffer! Oh, don't weep,
come back to being your father's pride and joy.

(Alfredo sits in despair at the table, his face in his hands.)

Di Provenza il mar, il suol,   [17]
chi dal cor ti cancellò?
Al natio fulgente sol
qual destino ti furò?
Oh, rammenta pur nel duol,
ch'ivi gioia a te brillò;
e che pace colà sol
su te splendere ancor può.
Dio mi guidò!

Ah, il tuo vecchio genitor,
tu non sai quanto soffrì…
Te lontano, di squallor
il suo tetto si coprì…
Ma se alfin ti trovo ancor,
se in me speme non fallì,
se la voce dell'onor
in te appien non ammutì,
Dio m'esaudì!

(abbracciandolo)

Né rispondi d'un padre all'affetto?

ALFREDO
Mille serpi divoranmi il petto…

(respingendo il padre)

Mi lasciate.

GERMONT
          Lasciarti!

ALFREDO *(risoluto)*
               (Oh, vendetta!)

GERMONT
Non più indugi, partiamo, t'affretta.

ALFREDO
(Ah, fu Douphol!)

What could have made you forget [17]
the sea and the soil of Provence?
What destiny has drawn you away
from the bright sunshine of your homeland?
Oh, even in your grief, remember
the happiness that shone on you there,
for only there can peace
smile on you again.
God has led me here!

Ah, you cannot know how much
your old father has suffered!
In your absence his house
has become desolate…
But if I have found you again,
if my hopes are not in vain,
if the voice of honour
is not entirely dead within you,
then God has heard my prayer!

(embracing him)

Won't you respond to your father's love?

ALFREDO
A thousand serpents are gnawing at my heart.

(repulsing his father)

Leave me alone!

GERMONT
                    Leave you!

ALFREDO *(with determination)*
                              (Oh, I shall be avenged!)

GERMONT
Do not delay further, let us go, make haste.

ALFREDO
(Ah, it was Douphol!)

GERMONT

M'ascolti tu?

ALFREDO

No!

GERMONT

Dunque invano trovato t'avrò?
No, non udrai rimproveri;
copriam d'oblio il passato:
L'amor che m'ha guidato
sa tutto perdonar.
Vieni, i tuoi cari in giubilo
con me rivedi ancora;
a chi penò finora
tal gioia non negar.
Un padre ed una suora
t'affretta a consolar.

ALFREDO

Mille serpi divoranmi il petto.

GERMONT

M'ascolti tu?

ALFREDO

No!

GERMONT

Un padre ed una suora
t'affretta a consolar, *ecc.*

ALFREDO *(Scuotendosi, getta a caso gli occhi sulla tavola, vede
la lettera di Flora, la scorre ed esclama)*
Ah!... Ell'è alla festa! Volisi
l'offesa a vendicar.

(Fugge precipitoso.)

GERMONT

Will you listen to me?

ALFREDO

No!

GERMONT
So have I found you again in vain?
No, you shall hear no reproaches;
let the past be completely forgotten:
the love that brought me here
can forgive everything.
Come, see again with me
your dear ones rejoicing;
don't deny that joy
to those who have suffered.
Hasten to console
your father and your sister.

ALFREDO
A thousand serpents are gnawing at my heart.

GERMONT
Will you listen to me?

ALFREDO
No!

GERMONT
Hasten to console
your father and your sister, *etc.*

ALFREDO *(pulling himself together, he chances to see Flora's letter on the table, reads it and bursts out)*
Ah! She's gone to that party!
I must hurry to avenge this.

(He rushes out.)

GERMONT

Che dici? Ah, ferma!

(Lo insegue.)

Scena IX

Galleria nel palazzo di Flora, riccamente addobbata e illuminata. Una porta nel fondo e due laterali. A destra più avanti un tavoliere con quanto occorre pel giuoco; a sinistra, ricco tavolino con fiori e rinfreschi, varie sedie e un divano.

(Flora, il Marchese, il Dottore ed altri invitati entrano dalla sinistra discorrendo fra loro.) [18]

FLORA

Avrem lieta di maschere la notte:
n'è duce il viscontino…
Violetta ed Alfredo anco invitai.

MARCHESE

La novità ignorate?
Violetta e Germont sono disgiunti.

DOTTORE e FLORA

Fia vero?…

MARCHESE

Ella verrà qui col Barone.

DOTTORE

Li vidi ieri ancor!… Parean felici.

(S'ode rumore a destra.)

FLORA

Silenzio!… Udite?…

TUTTI *(Vanno verso la destra.)*

Giungono gli amici!

Scena X

(Molte signore mascherate da Zingare entrano dalla destra.)

GERMONT

What are you saying? Stop!

(He follows him.)

Scene 9

A large hall in Flora's mansion, luxuriously furnished and brightly lit. A door at the back and one at either side. On the right, in the foreground, stands a table set apart for gambling; on the left is a table richly furnished with flowers and refreshments; there are several chairs and a divan.

(Flora, the Marquis, the Doctor and other guests enter in conversation from the door on the left.) [18]

FLORA
We have maskers to enliven the evening:
the young Vicomte is leading them.
I've also invited Violetta and Alfredo…

MARQUIS
Haven't you heard the news?
Violetta and Germont have separated.

DOCTOR and FLORA
Really?

MARQUIS
She's coming with the Baron.

DOCTOR
I saw them just yesterday! They seemed happy.

(A noise is heard from the right.)

FLORA
Quiet! Can you hear that?

ALL *(going towards the door on the right)*
Our friends have arrived!

Scene 10

(Several ladies masked as gypsies enter from the right.)

Coro di zingarelle

ZINGARELLE
>Noi siamo zingarelle   [19]
>venute da lontano;
>d'ognuno sulla mano
>leggiamo l'avvenir.
>Se consultiam le stelle
>null'avvi a noi d'oscuro
>e i casi del futuro
>possiamo altrui predir.

PRIME ZINGARELLE *(Prendono la mano di Flora e l'osservano.)*
>Vediamo! Voi, signora,
>rivali alquante avete.

SECONDE ZINGARELLE *(osservando la mano del Marchese)*
>Marchese, voi non siete
>model di fedeltà.

FLORA *(al Marchese)*
>Fate il galante ancora?
>Ben, vo' me la paghiate...

MARCHESE *(a Flora)*
>Che diamin vi pensate?...
>L'accusa è falsità!

FLORA
>La volpe lascia il pelo,
>non abbandona il vizio.
>Marchese mio, giudizio,
>o vi farò pentir!

TUTTI
>Su via, si stenda un velo
>sui fatti del passato;

Gypsies' Chorus

GYPSIES

We're gypsy girls   [19]
from far away;
we can read anyone's hand
and see what will come to pass.
When we search in the stars
nothing is hidden from us:
we can predict
what the future holds.

FIRST GROUP OF GYPSIES *(taking Flora's hand and*
examining her palm)
Let's see! You, Madame,
have several rivals.

SECOND GROUP OF GYPSIES *(examining the Marquis's palm)*
Marquis, you are not
a model of fidelity.

FLORA *(to the Marquis)*
Are you still up to your tricks?
Very well, you'll pay for that!

MARQUIS *(to Flora)*
How could you think that?
The accusation is quite false!

FLORA

The fox can change his coat,
but not his bad habits.
My dear Marquis, be careful,
or you'll be sorry!

ALL

Come on, let's draw a veil
over what's past;

già quel ch'è stato è stato,
badiamo *(badate)* all'avvenir.

(Flora ed il Marchese si stringono la mano.)

Scena XI

(Gastone ed altri mascherati da Mattadori e Piccadori spagnuoli entrano vivacemente dalla destra.)

Coro di mattadori spagnuoli

GASTONE e MATTADORI
Di Madride noi siam mattadori,
siamo i prodi del circo dei tori,
testé giunti a godere del chiasso
che a Parigi si fa pel bue grasso;
è una storia, se udire vorrete,
quali amanti noi siamo saprete.

FLORA, DOTTORE, MARCHESE, CORO DI DONNE
Sì, sì, bravi, narrate, narrate!
Con piacere l'udremo!

GASTONE e MATTADORI
                    Ascoltate.

È Piquillo un bel gagliardo   [20]
biscaglino mattador;
forte il braccio, fiero il guardo,
delle giostre egli è signor.
D'andalusa giovinetta
follemente innamorò;
ma la bella ritrosetta
così al giovane parlò:
'Cinque tori in un sol giorno
vo' vederti ad atterrar;
e, se vinci, al tuo ritorno
mano e cor ti vo' donar.'
Sì, gli disse, e il mattadore
alle giostre mosse il piè;

what's done is done,
let's look to the future.

(Flora and the Marquis shake hands.)

Scene 11

(Gaston and other maskers burst in from the right, dressed as Spanish matadors and picadors.)

Spanish Matadors' Chorus

GASTON and MATADORS
We're matadors from Madrid,
the heroes of the bullring,
we've just arrived to enjoy the fun
to be had in Paris with the Shrovetide bull.
And if you want to hear a story,
you'll find out what sort of lovers we are.

FLORA, DOCTOR, MARQUIS, CHORUS OF LADIES
Yes, yes, you fine fellows, tell us, tell us!
We'll listen with pleasure!

GASTON AND MATADORS
                    Listen!

Piquillo's a fine young man,   [20]
a matador from Biscay;
strong of arm, proud of gaze,
he's a master of the bullfight.
He fell madly in love
with an Andalusian girl,
but the fair girl played coy
and spoke to him thus:
'I want to see you strike down
five bulls in a single day;
if you come back victorious
I'll give you my hand and my heart.'
The matador agreed,
and set off for the bullring.

cinque tori, vincitore,
sull'arena egli stendé.

FLORA, DOTTORE, MARCHESE, CORO DI DONNE
Bravo, bravo il mattadore,
ben gagliardo si mostrò,
se alla giovane l'amore
in tal guisa egli provò!

GASTONE e MATTADORI
Poi, tra plausi, ritornato
alla bella del suo cor,
colse il premio desiato
tra le braccia dell'amor.

FLORA, DOTTORE, MARCHESE, FLORA, CORO DI DONNE
Con tai prove i mattadori
san le belle conquistar.

GASTONE e MATTADORI
Ma qui son più miti i cori;
a noi basta folleggiar.

TUTTI
Sì, allegri… Or pria tentiamo
della sorte il vario umor;
la palestra dischiudiamo
agli audaci giuocator.

(Gli uomini si tolgono la maschera: chi passeggia e chi si accinge a giuocare.)

Scena XII

(Entra Alfredo.)

TUTTI
Alfredo!… Voi!…

ALFREDO
Sì, amici.

Five bulls he triumphantly
stretched out on the ground.

FLORA, DOCTOR, MARQUIS, CHORUS OF LADIES
Bravo, bravo, the matador
showed himself to be a true gallant
if he proved his love
for the girl like that!

GASTON and MATADORS
Amidst the cheers of the crowd
he went back to the girl he loved
and gathered the reward he longed for
in the arms of his love.

FLORA, DOCTOR, MARQUIS, CHORUS OF LADIES
That's the way that matadors
conquer girls' hearts.

GASTON and MATADORS
But here your hearts are more tender;
we'll confine ourselves to merriment.

ALL
Yes, let's merrily see
how chance looks upon us;
let's open up the competition
to the bold gamblers.

(The men remove their masks; some wander around, others settle down to gambling.)

Scene 12

(Enter Alfredo)

ALL
Alfredo! You've come!

ALFREDO
                    Yes, my friends.

FLORA
Violetta?

ALFREDO
Non ne so.

TUTTI
Ben disinvolto!… Bravo!…
Or via, giuocar si può.

(Entra Violetta a braccio del Barone.)   [21]

FLORA *(andandole incontro)*
Qui desiata giungi!

VIOLETTA
Cessi al cortese invito.

FLORA
Grata vi son, Barone,
d'averlo pur gradito.

BARONE *(piano a Violetta)*
Germont è qui! Il vedete?

VIOLETTA
(Cielo! gli è vero!)

(piano al Barone)

Il vedo.

BARONE *(cupo)*
Da voi non un sol detto
si volga a questo Alfredo…
non un detto!

VIOLETTA
(Ah, perché venni, incauta!   [22]
Pietà, gran Dio, di me!)

FLORA
And Violetta?

ALFREDO
I don't know.

ALL
How nonchalant! Well done!
Now let's have a game.

(Violetta enters on the Baron's arm.) [21]

FLORA *(going to greet them)*
We were so looking forward to seeing you!

VIOLETTA
I couldn't refuse your lovely invitation.

FLORA
I'm also grateful to you,
Baron, for coming.

BARON *(quietly, to Violetta)*
Germont is here! Do you see him?

VIOLETTA
(Heavens, so he is!)

(quietly to the Baron)

I do.

BARON *(darkly)*
You mustn't utter
a single word to Alfredo...
not a word!

VIOLETTA
(Ah, why was I so rash as to come? [22]
Have mercy on me, Lord!)

FLORA *(a Violetta, facendola sedere presso di sé sul divano)*
  Meco t'assidi; narrami:
  quai novità vegg'io?

(Il Dottore si avvicina ad esse, che sommessamente conversano. Il Marchese si trattiene a parte col Barone; Gastone taglia, Alfredo ed altri puntano, altri passeggiano.)

ALFREDO
  Un quattro!

GASTONE
          Ancora hai vinto.

ALFREDO *(Punta e vince.)*
  Sfortuna nell'amore
  fortuna reca al giuoco!…

GASTONE, MARCHESE, CORO DI UOMINI
  È sempre vincitore!…

ALFREDO
  Oh, vincerò stasera,
  e l'oro guadagnato
  poscia a goder fra' campi
  ritornerò beato.

FLORA
  Solo?

ALFREDO
      No, no, con tale
  che vi fu meco ancora,
  poi mi sfuggia…

VIOLETTA
          (Mio Dio!)

GASTONE *(ad Alfredo indicando Violetta)*
  Pietà di lei!

BARONE *(ad Alfredo con mal frenata ira)*
          Signor!

FLORA *(to Violetta, inviting her to sit beside her on the divan)*
    Sit beside me, tell me all
    about this new state of affairs.

(The Doctor approaches them as they quietly speak together; the Marquis and the Baron stand apart in conversation; Gaston cuts the cards, Alfredo and others place their stakes, others pass to and fro.)

ALFREDO
    Four!

GASTON
        You've won again.

ALFREDO *(placing his stake and winning)*
    Unlucky in love,
    lucky at cards...

GASTON, MARQUIS, CHORUS OF MEN
    He keeps on winning!

ALFREDO
    Ah, this evening I shall win,
    and then I shall return
    happily to the country
    to enjoy my winnings.

FLORA
    Alone?

ALFREDO
        No, no, with the woman
    who used to be with me
    until she ran off.

VIOLETTA
            (O God!)

GASTON *(to Alfredo, indicating Violetta)*
    Be kind to her.

BARON *(to Alfredo, barely concealing his anger)*
            Sir!

VIOLETTA *(piano al Barone)*
Frenatevi o vi lascio.

ALFREDO *(disinvolto)*
Barone m'appellaste?

BARONE
Siete in sì gran fortuna,
che al giuoco mi tentaste…

ALFREDO *(ironico)*
Sì?… La disfida accetto…

VIOLETTA
(Che fia? Morir mi sento!
Pietà, gran Dio, di me!)

BARONE *(puntando)*
Cento luigi a destra.

ALFREDO *(puntando)*
Ed alla manca cento.

GASTONE *(tagliando)*
Un asso… un fante…

(ad Alfredo)

Hai vinto!

BARONE
Il doppio?

ALFREDO
Il doppio sia.

GASTONE *(tagliando)*
Un quattro, un sette.

DOTTORE, MARCHESE, INVITI
Ancora!

ALFREDO
Pur la vittoria è mia!

VIOLETTA *(quietly, to the Baron)*
Control yourself, or I shall leave you.

ALFREDO *(nonchalantly)*
Did you address me, Baron?

BARON
You're having such good fortune
that I'm temped to try my luck...

ALFREDO *(ironically)*
Indeed? I accept your challenge.

VIOLETTA
(What will happen? I could die!
Have mercy on me, Lord!)

BARON *(staking)*
A hundred louis on the right...

ALFREDO *(staking)*
And a hundred on the left...

GASTON *(cutting the cards)*
Ace... jack...

(to Alfredo)

You've won!

BARON
Double the stakes?

ALFREDO
Very well, double.

GASTON *(cutting)*
Four... seven...

DOCTOR, MARQUIS, GUESTS
Again!

ALFREDO
So I've won!

GASTONE, DOTTORE, MARCHESE, INVITI
Bravo davver!... La sorte
è tutta per Alfredo!...

FLORA
Del villeggiar la spesa
farà il Baron, già il vedo.

ALFREDO *(al Barone)*
Seguite pur!

(Entra un servo.)

SERVO
           La cena
è pronta.

FLORA
      Andiamo, andiamo.

TUTTI *(avviandosi)*
Andiamo, andiam.

VIOLETTA
(Che fia? Morir mi sento!
Pietà, gran Dio, di me!)

ALFREDO *(al Barone)*
Se continuar v'aggrada...

BARONE
Per ora nol possiamo:
più tardi la rivincita.

ALFREDO
Al giuoco che vorrete.

BARONE
Seguiam gli amici; poscia...

ALFREDO
Sarò qual bramerete.

GASTON, DOCTOR, MARQUIS, GUESTS
Well done! Alfredo
is really in luck!

FLORA
I can see it's the Baron who'll be paying
for that stay in the country.

ALFREDO *(to the Baron)*
Shall we continue?

(A servant appears.)

SERVANT
                    Supper
is served.

FLORA
            Let's go, let's go.

ALL *(moving away)*
Let's go, let's go.

VIOLETTA
(What will happen? I could die!
Have mercy on me, Lord!)

ALFREDO *(to the Baron)*
If you'd like to continue…

BARON
We can't do so now;
We'll play again later.

ALFREDO
At any game you wish.

BARON
Let's follow our friends… later…

ALFREDO
I am at your service.

(Si allontanano.)

Andiam.

BARONE *(ben lontano)*

Andiam.

(Tutti entrano nella porta di mezzo, la scena rimane un istante vuota.)

Scena XIII

(Violetta ritorna affannata.)

VIOLETTA
Invitato a qui seguirmi,
verrà desso?… vorrà udirmi?…
Ei verrà… ché l'odio atroce
puote in lui più di mia voce…

ALFREDO *(entrando)*
Mi chiamaste? Che bramate?

VIOLETTA
Questi luoghi abbandonate…
un periglio vi sovrasta…

ALFREDO
Ah, comprendo… Basta, basta…
E sì vile mi credete?

VIOLETTA
Ah no, mai…

ALFREDO
Ma che temete?

VIOLETTA
Tremo sempre del Barone…

ALFREDO
È fra noi mortal quistione…
S'ei cadrà per mano mia,
un sol colpo vi torria

(They move away.)

Let's go.

BARON *(further away)*

Let's go.

(Everyone goes out by the central door; the room is empty for a moment.)

Scene 13

(Violetta returns, greatly agitated.)

VIOLETTA
I asked him to follow me here,
will he come now? Will he listen to me?
He'll come. The terrible hatred he's feeling
will move him more than anything I could say…

ALFREDO *(entering)*
You asked to see me? What do you want?

VIOLETTA
Leave this house;
danger threatens you!

ALFREDO
Ah, I understand. Enough, enough.
Do you think me so cowardly?

VIOLETTA
Ah no, never!

ALFREDO

So what are you afraid of?

VIOLETTA
I'm frightened of the Baron.

ALFREDO
There is a deadly quarrel between us.
If he falls by my hand,
you will be deprived at a stroke

coll'amante il protettore…
V'atterrisce tal sciagura?

VIOLETTA
Ma s'ei fosse l'uccisore!…
Ecco l'unica sventura
ch'io pavento a me fatale.

ALFREDO
La mia morte!… Che ven cale?

VIOLETTA
Deh, partite, e sull'istante!

ALFREDO
Partirò, ma giura innante
che dovunque seguirai,
i miei passi…

VIOLETTA
                    Ah! no, giammai!

ALFREDO
No! giammai!…

VIOLETTA
                    Va', sciagurato.
Scorda un nome ch'è infamato.
Va'… mi lascia sul momento…
Di fuggirti un giuramento
sacro io feci…

ALFREDO
                    E chi potea?

VIOLETTA
A chi dritto pien n'avea.

ALFREDO
Fu Douphol?

VIOLETTA *(con supremo sforzo)*
                    Sì.

of your lover and your protector.
Does such a catastrophe terrify you?

VIOLETTA
But suppose he kills you?…
That is the only outcome
that makes me mortally afraid.

ALFREDO
My death!… What does that matter to you?

VIOLETTA
Please go, go at once!

ALFREDO
I shall go, but first you must swear
that wherever you go, you will
follow me…

VIOLETTA
   Ah, no! Never!

ALFREDO
No? Never?

VIOLETTA
   Go, wretched man!
Forget my dishonourable name!
Go, leave me at once!
I swore a solemn oath
to fly from you.

ALFREDO
   Tell me, who made you swear it?

VIOLETTA
Someone who had every right to do so.

ALFREDO
Was it Douphol?

VIOLETTA *(making an extreme effort)*
   Yes.

ALFREDO
                    Dunque l'ami?

VIOLETTA
    Ebben... l'amo...

ALFREDO *(Corre furente sulla porta e grida.)*
                    Or tutti a me.

Scena XIV

(Tutti entrano confusamente.)

FLORA, GASTONE, BARONE, DOTTORE, MARCHESE,
    INVITI
    Ne appellaste?... Che volete?

ALFREDO *(additando Violetta che abbattuta si appoggia al tavolino)*
    Questa donna conoscete?

TUTTI
    Chi?... Violetta?

ALFREDO
                    Che facesse
    non sapete?

VIOLETTA
                Ah! taci!

TUTTI
                    No.

ALFREDO
    Ogni suo aver tal femmina
    per amor mio sperdea...
    Io cieco, vile, misero,
    tutto accettar potea,
    ma è tempo ancora!... tergermi
    da tanta macchia bramo...
    Qui or testimon vi chiamo
    che qui pagata io l'ho.

ALFREDO
                    Do you love him, then?

VIOLETTA
    Yes… I love him…

ALFREDO *(furiously running to the door and calling out)*
    Come in here, all of you!

Scene 14

(All the guests crowd back into the room.)

FLORA, GASTON, BARON, DOCTOR, MARQUIS,
    GUESTS
    You called us? What is it?

ALFREDO *(pointing to Violetta, who is leaning desolately*
    against the table)
    Do you know this woman?

ALL
    Who? Violetta?

ALFREDO
                    Don't you know
    what she did?

VIOLETTA
            Ah! Be quiet!

ALL
                    No.

ALFREDO
    This woman spent everything she had
    because she loved me…
    I was blind, I behaved like a wretched coward
    and accepted it all.
    But now the time has come for me
    to clear myself of such a disgrace.
    I call you all to witness
    that I've paid her back.

(Getta con furente sprezzo una borsa ai piedi di Violetta, che sviene fra le braccia di Flora. In tal momento entra il padre di Alfredo.)

Scena XV

GASTONE, BARONE, DOTTORE, MARCHESE, INVITI
 Oh, infamia orribile tu commettesti!...   [23]
 Un cor sensibile così uccidesti!...
 Di donne ignobile insultatore,
 di qua allontanati, ne desti orror.
 Va'!

GERMONT *(con dignitoso fuoco)*
 Di sprezzo degno se stesso rende
 chi pur nell'ira la donna offende.
 Dov'è mio figlio?... Più non lo vedo;
 in te più Alfredo trovar non so.

ALFREDO
 (Ah sì!... che feci!... Ne sento orrore.
 Gelosa smania, deluso amore
 mi strazian l'alma... più non ragiono.
 Da lei perdono più non avrò.
 Volea fuggirla... non ho potuto.
 Dall'ira spinto son qui venuto!
 Or che lo sdegno ho disfogato,
 me sciagurato! rimorso n'ho!)

FLORA, GASTONE, DOTTORE, MARCHESE, INVITI *(a Violetta)*
 Oh, quanto peni!... Ma pur fa cor...   [24]
 Qui soffre ognuno del tuo dolor;
 fra cari amici qui sei soltanto,
 rasciuga il pianto che t'inondò.

GERMONT
 (Io sol fra tanti, so qual virtude
 di quella misera il sen racchiude...
 Io so che l'ama, che gli è fedele;
 eppur crudele tacer dovrò!)

(With a gesture of furious contempt, he throws his winnings at Violetta's feet. She faints into Flora's arms. At this moment Alfredo's father appears.)

Scene 15

GASTON, BARON, DOCTOR, MARQUIS, GUESTS
 Ah, you have committed a disgraceful outrage!   [23]
 To destroy a tender heart with such behaviour!
 You have shamefully insulted a woman:
 get out of here – you fill us with horror!
 Go!

GERMONT *(with dignified anger)*
 A man who insults a woman, even in anger,
 is himself worthy only of contempt.
 Where is my son? I do not see him;
 Alfredo, I no longer recognize you.

ALFREDO
 (Ah yes! What have I done? I'm horrified!
 Jealous rage, disappointed love,
 are tearing at my heart, destroying my reason.
 She will never be able to forgive me.
 I wanted to fly from her, but I couldn't.
 I came here driven by my rage!
 Now that I've vented my anger
 I feel wretchedly ashamed!)

FLORA, GASTON, DOCTOR, MARQUIS, GUESTS *(to Violetta)*
 Oh, how you have suffered! But take heart!   [24]
 Everyone here sympathizes with your sorrow;
 you are among dear friends here,
 dry the tears that you are shedding.

GERMONT
 (Among all these people, I alone know what goodness
 the unhappy woman hides within her heart...
 I know how she loves him, how she is faithful to him,
 and yet I must cruelly keep silent.)

BARONE *(piano ad Alfredo)*
A questa donna l'atroce insulto
qui tutti offese, ma non inulto
fia tanto oltraggio… Provar vi voglio
che il vostro orgoglio fiaccar saprò.

ALFREDO
Ohimè, che feci! Ne sento orrore!
Da lei perdono più non avrò.

VIOLETTA *(riavendosi)*
Alfredo, Alfredo, di questo core   [25]
non puoi comprendere tutto l'amore,
tu non conosci che fino a prezzo
del tuo disprezzo provato io l'ho.

FLORA, GASTONE, DOTTORE, MARCHESE, INVITI
Quanto peni, *ecc.*

ALFREDO
Ohimè, che feci! *ecc.*

BARONE
Provar vi voglio, *ecc.*
A questa donna l'atroce insulto, *ecc.*

VIOLETTA
Ma verrà tempo, in che il saprai…
come t'amassi, confesserai…
Dio dai rimorsi ti salvi allora!
Ah! Io spenta ancora, pur t'amerò.

GERMONT
Io so che l'ama, *ecc.*

(Germont trae seco il figlio; il Barone lo segue. Violetta è condotta in altra stanza dal Dottore e da Flora: gli altri si disperdono.)

BARON *(quietly, to Alfredo)*
Your atrocious insult to this lady
has offended everyone, but such an outrage
shall not go unavenged. I wish to challenge you:
I shall know how to humble your pride.

ALFREDO
Alas, what have I done? I'm horrified!
She will never be able to forgive me.

VIOLETTA *(recovering)*
Alfredo, Alfredo, you cannot understand   [25]
the love there is in my heart;
you do not know that I have given proof of it,
even at the cost of inviting your contempt.

FLORA, GASTON, DOCTOR, MARQUIS, GUESTS
How you have suffered, *etc.*

ALFREDO
Alas, what have I done, *etc.*

BARON
I wish to challenge you, *etc.*
Your atrocious insult to this lady, *etc.*

VIOLETTA
But the time will come when you will know...
you will have to admit how much I loved you...
May God spare you then from remorse!
Ah, I shall love you even when I am dead.

GERMONT
I know she loves him, *etc.*

(Germont leads his son away, the Baron follows them. Flora and the Doctor take Violetta into the other room; the remaining guests disperse.)

ATTO TERZO

Preludio [1]

Scena I

Camera da letto di Violetta. Nel fondo è un letto con cortine mezze tirate; una finestra chiusa da imposte interne; presso il letto uno sgabello su cui una bottiglia di acqua, una tazza di cristallo, diverse medicine. A metà della scena una toilette, vicino un canapè; più distante un altro mobile, su cui arde un lume da notte; varie sedie ed altri mobili. La porta è a sinistra; di fronte v'è un caminetto con fuoco acceso.

(Violetta dorme sul letto; Annina, seduta presso il caminetto è pure addormentata.)

VIOLETTA *(destandosi)*
Annina?

ANNINA *(destandosi confusa)*
Comandate?

VIOLETTA
Dormivi? poveretta!

ANNINA
Sì, perdonate!

VIOLETTA
Dammi d'acqua un sorso.

(Annina eseguisce.)

Osserva, è pieno il giorno?

164

ACT THREE

Prelude [1]

[1]

Scene 1

Violetta's bedroom. At the back is a bed with the curtains half-drawn. There is a closed window with shutters on the inside; beside the bed a small table with a bottle of water, a crystal glass and various medicines on it. In the centre is a dressing table and near it a sofa. Further away, another table with a burning night light; other furniture and some chairs. The door is on the left. Opposite is a fireplace with a fire burning in it.

(Violetta is asleep on the bed; Annina, seated by the fireplace, is also dozing.)

VIOLETTA *(waking up)*
  Annina?

ANNINA *(waking in confusion)*
          Yes, Madame?

VIOLETTA
  Were you asleep? Poor Annina!

ANNINA
  Yes, forgive me!

VIOLETTA
          Give me a sip of water.

(Annina does so.)

  Look and see if it's daylight.

ANNINA

Son sett'ore.

VIOLETTA
Dà accesso a un po' di luce.

ANNINA *(Apre le imposte e guarda nella via.)*
Il signor di Grenvil…

VIOLETTA

Oh, il vero amico!…
Alzar mi vo'… m'aita.

(Si alza e ricade; poi, sostenuta da Annina, va lentamente verso il canapè, ed il Dottore entra in tempo per assisterla ad adagiarvisi. Annina vi aggiunge dei cuscini.)

Scena II

VIOLETTA
Quanta bontà!… Pensaste a me per tempo!…

DOTTORE *(Le tocca il polso.)*
Sì, come vi sentite?

VIOLETTA
Soffre il mio corpo, ma tranquilla ho l'alma.
Mi confortò ier sera un pio ministro.
Religione è sollievo ai sofferenti.

DOTTORE
E questa notte?

VIOLETTA

Ebbi tranquillo il sonno.

DOTTORE
Coraggio adunque… la convalescenza
non è lontana…

VIOLETTA

Oh, la bugia pietosa
ai medici è concessa…

ANNINA

It's seven o'clock.

VIOLETTA
Let some light in.

ANNINA *(opening the shutters and looking into the street)*
Monsieur de Grenvil…

VIOLETTA

Oh, what a good friend he's been!
I want to get up… help me.

(She rises, but falls back. Then with Annina's help she goes slowly to the sofa. The Doctor arrives in time to help her and make her comfortable. Annina brings some cushions.)

Scene 2

VIOLETTA
How good you are! To think of me so early!

DOCTOR *(feeling her pulse)*
Yes. How are you feeling?

VIOLETTA
My body is in pain, but my soul is at peace.
A good priest came yesterday evening to comfort me..
Religion is a great solace when you're ill.

DOCTOR
And last night?

VIOLETTA

I slept peacefully.

DOCTOR
Then take heart, you will soon
be convalescent.

VIOLETTA

Oh, Doctors are allowed
to tell comforting lies…

DOTTORE *(stringendole la mano)*
> Addio… a più tardi!

VIOLETTA
Non mi scordate.

ANNINA *(piano al Dottore accompagnandolo)*
> Come va, signore?

DOTTORE *(piano a parte)*
La tisi non le accorda che poche ore.

(Esce.)

Scena III

ANNINA *(a Violetta)*
Or fate cor!

VIOLETTA
> Giorno di festa è questo?

ANNINA
Tutta Parigi impazza… è carnevale.

VIOLETTA
Ah, nel comun tripudio, sallo Iddio,
quanti infelici soffron!… Quale somma
v'ha in quello stipo?

(indicandolo)

ANNINA *(Apre e conta.)*
> Venti luigi.

VIOLETTA
> > Dieci
ne reca a' poveri tu stessa.

ANNINA
> > Poco
rimanvi allora…

DOCTOR *(shaking her hand)*
>Goodbye, I'll visit you later.

VIOLETTA
Don't forget me.

ANNINA *(quietly, while showing the Doctor to the door)*
>How is she, sir?

DOCTOR *(quietly, aside to Annina)*
The consumption will only spare her for a few more hours.

(He leaves.)

Scene 3

ANNINA *(to Violetta)*
Now be brave!

VIOLETTA
>Is today a holiday?

ANNINA
All Paris has gone wild... it's Carnival.

VIOLETTA
Ah, God alone knows how many wretched people
are suffering while all the others enjoy themselves. How much
is there in that drawer?

(pointing to it)

ANNINA *(opening it and counting the money)*
>Twenty louis.

VIOLETTA
>Take ten,
and give them yourself to the poor.

ANNINA
>You won't have
very much left then...

VIOLETTA
Oh, mi saran bastanti!
Cerca poscia mie lettere.

ANNINA
Ma voi?…

VIOLETTA
Null'occorrà… Sollecita, se puoi…

(Annina esce.)

Scena IV

VIOLETTA *(Trae dal seno una lettera e legge.)*
'Teneste la promessa… La disfida
ebbe luogo. Il Barone fu ferito,
però migliora… Alfredo
è in stranio suolo. Il vostro sacrifizio
io stesso gli ho svelato;
egli a voi tornerà pel suo perdono;
io pur verrò… Curatevi… Mertate
un avvenir migliore.
Giorgio Germont.'

(desolata)

È tardi!…

(Si alza.)

Attendo, attendo… né a me giungon mai!…

(Si guarda nello specchio.)

Oh, come son mutata!
Ma il Dottore a sperar pure m'esorta!
Ah! con tal morbo ogni speranza è morta!

Addio del passato bei sogni ridenti,   [26]
le rose del volto già sono pallenti;
l'amore d'Alfredo perfino mi manca,
conforto, sostegno dell'anima stanca…

VIOLETTA

Oh, it'll be enough for me!
Then see if there are any letters.

ANNINA

But what about yourself?

VIOLETTA

I don't need anything... Hurry, if you can...

(Annina leaves.)

Scene 4

VIOLETTA *(taking a letter from her breast and reading it)*   [6]
'You have kept your promise... The duel
took place, the Baron was wounded,
but is now recovering... Alfredo
has gone abroad. I myself
have told him of your sacrifice;
he is coming back to beg your forgiveness;
I shall come too. Take care of yourself... You deserve
a better future.
Georges Germont.'

(sadly)

Too late!

(She rises.)

I've been waiting and waiting, but they never come!

(She looks at herself in the mirror.)

Oh, how I've changed!
But the Doctor encourages me to keep hoping!
Ah, with this disease all hope is dead!

Farewell to those happy dreams of bygone days,   [26]
the roses of my cheeks are already faded.
I am even left without Alfredo's love
to comfort and strengthen my weary spirit...

Ah, della traviata sorridi al desio;
a lei, deh, perdona, tu accoglila, o Dio!
Ah! Tutto finì, or tutto finì.

Le gioie, i dolori tra poco avran fine,
la tomba ai mortali di tutto è confine!
Non lacrima o fiore avrà la mia fossa,
non croce col nome che copra quest'ossa!
Ah, della traviata sorridi al desio, *ecc.*

CORO DI MASCHERE *(all'esterno)*
   Largo al quadrupede   [27]
   sir della festa,
   di fiori e pampini
   cinta la testa.
   Largo al più docile
   d'ogni cornuto,
   di corni e pifferi
   abbia il saluto.
   Parigini, date passo
   al trionfo del bue grasso.

   L'Asia, né l'Africa
   vide il più bello,
   vanto ed orgoglio
   d'ogni macello.
   Allegre maschere,
   pazzi garzoni,
   tutti plauditelo
   con canti e suoni!
   Parigini, date passo
   al trionfo del bue grasso.

Scena V

(Annina torna frettolosa.)

ANNINA *(esitando)*
   Signora…

O God, look kindly upon the longings of a fallen woman,
grant her forgiveness, take her to yourself!
Ah! It's all over, all over now.

All joys and sorrows will soon come to an end;
the tomb waits to receive every mortal!
No tears or flowers will deck my grave,
no cross with my name on it will show where my bones lie!
O God, look kindly upon the longings, *etc.*

CHORUS OF MASKERS *(from the street)*

Make way for the four-footed   [27]
lord of the feast –
his head wreathed
with flowers and vines!
Make way for the gentlest
of horned animals –
greet him
with horns and pipes,
Parisians, make way
for the triumph of the fatted ox!

Nothing finer was ever seen
in Asia or in Africa:
he'd be the pride and joy
of any slaughterhouse!
Cheerful maskers,
wild boys,
come all of you and applaud him
with singing and music!
Parisians, make way
for the triumph of the fatted ox!

Scene 5

(Annina hurries back.)

ANNINA *(hesitantly)*
Madame...

VIOLETTA
Che t'accade?

ANNINA
Quest'oggi, è vero? vi sentite meglio?

VIOLETTA
Sì, perché?

ANNINA
D'esser calma promettete?

VIOLETTA
Sì, che vuoi dirmi?

ANNINA
Prevenir vi volli…
una gioia improvvisa.

VIOLETTA
Una gioia… dicesti?…

ANNINA
Sì, o signora.

VIOLETTA
Alfredo!… Ah, tu il vedesti!…
Ei vien!… L'affretta!

(Annina afferma col capo, e va ad aprire la porta.)

Scena VI

VIOLETTA *(andando verso l'uscio)*
Alfredo?

(Alfredo compare pallido per la commozione, ed ambedue si gettano le braccia al collo.)

Amato Alfredo, oh gioia!

ALFREDO
O mia Violetta, oh gioia!
Colpevol sono… so tutto, o cara!

VIOLETTA
What is it?

ANNINA
You are feeling better today, aren't you?

VIOLETTA
Yes, why?

ANNINA
Will you promise to keep calm?

VIOLETTA
Yes, what are you trying to tell me?

ANNINA
I want to prepare you
for a joy you weren't expecting.

VIOLETTA
A joy, did you say?

ANNINA
Yes, Madame.

VIOLETTA
Alfredo! Ah, you've seen him!
He's coming! Hurry!

(Annina nods and goes to open the door.)

Scene 6

VIOLETTA *(going to the door)*
Alfredo?

(Alfredo appears, pale with emotion, and they throw themselves into each other's arms.)

Beloved Alfredo, oh what joy!

ALFREDO
O my Violetta, what joy!
I feel so guilty... I know everything, my beloved!

VIOLETTA
Io so che alfine reso mi sei!

ALFREDO
Da questo palpito, s'io t'amo impara,
senza te esistere più non potrei.

VIOLETTA
Ah s'anco in vita m'hai ritrovata,
credi che uccidere non può il dolor.

ALFREDO
Scorda l'affanno, donna adorata,
a me perdona e al genitor.

VIOLETTA
Ch'io ti perdoni? La rea son io;
ma solo amor tal mi rendé.

ALFREDO, poi **VIOLETTA**
Null'uomo o demone, angelo mio,
mai più dividermi potrà da te.

ALFREDO
Parigi, o cara, noi lasceremo,   [28]
la vita uniti trascorreremo.
De' corsi affanni compenso avrai,
la tua salute rifiorirà.
Sospiro e luce tu mi sarai,
tutto il futuro ne arriderà.

VIOLETTA
Parigi, o caro, noi lasceremo,
la vita uniti trascorreremo.

ALFREDO
Sì.

VIOLETTA
De' corsi affanni compenso avrai,
la mia salute rifiorirà.

VIOLETTA
I know only that you've come back to me at last!

ALFREDO
Feel how I love you from the beating of my heart:
I can't live without you any longer.

VIOLETTA
Ah, if you find me alive,
it means that grief couldn't kill me.

ALFREDO
Forget your troubles, my beloved,
forgive me and forgive my father.

VIOLETTA
Why should I forgive you? I was the guilty one,
but it was love alone that made me so.

ALFREDO, then VIOLETTA
My angel, no man or demon
will ever separate me from you again.

ALFREDO
My love, we shall leave Paris   [28]
and live our lives together.
You will have your reward for past sufferings,
you will regain your health.
You will be the breath, the light of my life,
the future will smile on us.

VIOLETTA
My love, we shall leave Paris
and live our lives together.

ALFREDO
Yes.

VIOLETTA
You will have your reward for past sufferings,
I shall regain my health.

Sospiro e luce tu mi sarai,
tutto il futuro ne arriderà.

ALFREDO
Sospir, luce sarai.

ALFREDO e VIOLETTA
Parigi, o cara, noi lasceremo, *ecc.*

VIOLETTA
Ah, non più! A un tempio, Alfredo, andiamo,
del tuo ritorno grazie rendiamo.

(Vacilla.)

ALFREDO
Tu impallidisci!…

VIOLETTA
È nulla, sai?
Gioia improvvisa non entra mai,
senza turbarlo, in mesto core.

(Si abbandona sfinita sopra una sedia.)

ALFREDO *(spaventato sorreggendola)*
Gran Dio!… Violetta!…

VIOLETTA
È il mio malore!

(sforzandosi)

Fu debolezza!… Ora son forte.
Vedi? Sorrido…

ALFREDO *(desolato)*
(Ahi, cruda sorte!)

VIOLETTA
Fu nulla… Annina, dammi a vestire.

ALFREDO
Adesso?… Attendi…

You will be the breath, the light of my life,
the future will smile on us.

ALFREDO
You will be the breath, the light of my life, *etc.*

ALFREDO, VIOLETTA
My love, we shall leave Paris, *etc.*

VIOLETTA
Ah, no more! Let's go to church, Alfredo,
and give thanks for your return.

(She sways.)

ALFREDO
You've turned pale!

VIOLETTA
                 It's nothing, really.
A sudden joy is bound to cause
trouble in a sad heart.

(She falls exhausted onto a chair.)

ALFREDO *(frightened, supporting her)*
Dear God! Violetta!

VIOLETTA
                It's my illness!

(making an effort)

A moment of weakness! I'm stronger now
See? I'm smiling.

ALFREDO *(sadly)*
              (Ah, what a cruel fate!)

VIOLETTA
It was nothing! Annina, bring my clothes.

ALFREDO
Now? Wait for a moment…

VIOLETTA *(alzandosi)*
>No! Voglio uscire.

(Annina presenta a Violetta una veste ch'ella fa per indossare, ed impeditane dalla debolezza la getta a terra.)

Gran Dio! Non posso!

(Ricade sulla sedia.)

ALFREDO
>(Cielo!... che vedo!...)

(ad Annina)

Va' pel Dottore!

VIOLETTA *(ad Annina)*
>Digli che Alfredo
è ritornato all'amor mio,
digli che vivere ancor vogl'io...

(Annina parte.)

(ad Alfredo)

Ma se tornando non m'hai salvato,
a niuno in terra salvarmi è dato.

(sorgendo impetuosa)

Gran Dio! Morir sì giovine,   [29]
io che penato ho tanto!
Morir sì presso a tergere
il mio sì lungo pianto!
Ah, dunque fu delirio
la credula speranza;
invano di costanza
armato avrò il mio cor!

ALFREDO
Oh, mio sospiro e palpito,
diletto del cor mio!...

VIOLETTA *(rising)*

No! I want to go out.

(Annina brings Violetta a dress, which she tries to put on; but she is too weak to do so, and throws it to the ground.)

Dear God, I can't do it!

(She falls back on the chair.)

ALFREDO

(Heavens, to see her like this!)

(to Annina)

Go and fetch the Doctor!

VIOLETTA *(to Annina)*

Ah, tell him that Alfredo
has returned to my love –
tell him I want to live longer!

(Annina leaves.)

(to Alfredo)

But if your return hasn't saved me,
No one else on earth can do so.

(rising impetuously)

Ah! Dear God, to die so young   [29]
after all that I've suffered!
To die when I'm so close to recovering
from my days of weeping!
Ah, so my naive hope
was only an illusion;
it was all in vain, the constancy
with which I steeled my heart!

ALFREDO
Oh, breath and pulse of my life,
joy of my heart!

Le mie colle tue lagrime
confondere degg'io…
Ma più che mai, deh! credilo,
m'è d'uopo di costanza.
Ah! tutto alla speranza
non chiudere il tuo cor!

VIOLETTA
Oh, Alfredo, il crudo termine
serbato al nostro amor!
Gran Dio! Morir sì giovine!

ALFREDO
Violetta mia, deh! calmati,
m'uccide il tuo dolor!

(Violetta s'abbatte sul canapè.)

Scene 7

GERMONT *(entrando con Annina ed il Dottore)*
Ah, Violetta!

VIOLETTA
Voi, signor!

ALFREDO
Mio padre!

VIOLETTA
Non mi scordaste?

GERMONT
La promessa adempio…
A stringervi qual figlia vengo al seno,
o generosa…

VIOLETTA
Ahimè! Tardi giungeste!

(abbracciandolo)

Let me mingle my tears
with yours…
But believe me, more than ever
I need your devotion.
Ah, do not close your heart
to all hope!

VIOLETTA
Oh, Alfredo, this is the cruel end
destined to our love!
Ah! Dear God, to die so young!

ALFREDO
Ah! My Violetta, be calm,
your pain is killing me!

(Violetta collapses onto the sofa.)

Scene 7

GERMONT *(entering with Annina and the Doctor)*
Ah, Violetta!

VIOLETTA
It's you, Monsieur?

ALFREDO
Father!

VIOLETTA
So you didn't forget me?

GERMONT
I am fulfilling my promise:
to press you to my heart as a daughter,
generous girl.

VIOLETTA
Alas, you have arrived too late!

(embracing him)

Pure grata ven sono.
Grenvil, vedete? Fra le braccia spiro
di quanti cari ho al mondo.

GERMONT

Che mai dite!

(osservando Violetta)

(O cielo!… è ver!)

ALFREDO

La vedi, padre mio?

GERMONT
Di più non lacerarmi,
troppo rimorso l'alma mi divora…
Quasi fulmin m'atterra ogni suo detto…

(Violetta apre un ripostiglio e ne toglie un medaglione.)

Oh, malcauto vegliardo!
Ah, tutto il mal ch'io feci ora sol vedo!

VIOLETTA
Più a me t'appressa, ascolta, amato Alfredo.
Prendi, quest'è l'immagine
de' miei passati giorni,
a rammentar ti torni
colei che sì t'amò.

ALFREDO
No, non morrai, non dirmelo…
Dêi viver, amor mio…
A strazio sì terribile
qui non mi trasse Iddio…

GERMONT
Cara, sublime vittima
d'un disperato amore,
perdonami lo strazio
recato al tuo bel cor.

But I am still grateful.
You see, Doctor Grenvil? I'm dying in the arms
of those I hold dearest in the world.

GERMONT

Whatever are you saying?

(looking closely at Violetta)

(Heavens... she's right!)

ALFREDO

You see how she is, father?

GERMONT
Don't torture me any more,
my heart is too eaten up with remorse...
Every word she utters strikes me like a thunderbolt.

(Violetta opens a drawer and takes out a medallion.)

Ah, rash old man!
I realize only now how much harm I've caused!

VIOLETTA
Come closer, listen to me, darling Alfredo.
Take this, it shows me
as I used to be, in the past:
let it serve to remind you
of someone who loved you so much.

ALFREDO
No, don't die, don't say that...
You have to live, my love...
God would never have brought me here
to suffer such a terrible blow.

GERMONT
Dear, sublime victim
of a desperate love,
forgive me for the blow
I struck at your noble heart.

VIOLETTA

    Se una pudica vergine   [30]
    degli anni suoi sul fiore
    a te donasse il core…
    sposa ti sia… lo vo'.

    Le porgi quest'effigie;
    dille che dono ell'è
    di chi nel ciel fra gli angeli
    prega per lei, per te.

GERMONT, ANNINA, DOTTORE

    Finché avrà il ciglio lagrime
    io piangerò per te.
    Vola a' beati spiriti,
    Iddio ti chiama a sé.

ALFREDO

    Sì presto, ah no, dividerti
    morte non può da me.
    Ah, vivi, o solo un feretro
    m'accoglierà con te.

VIOLETTA

    Le porgi quest'effigie, *ecc.*

(rialzandosi animata)

    È strano!…

ANNINA, ALFREDO, GERMONT, DOTTORE
          Che?

VIOLETTA

              Cessarono
    gli spasmi del dolore!
    In me rinasce, m'agita
    insolito vigor!
    Ah! ma io ritorno a vivere…
    Oh gioia!

(Ricade sul canapè.)

VIOLETTA

If some pure-hearted girl [30]
in the flower of her youth
should give you her heart…
let her be your wife… it's what I'd want.

Show her this picture;
say that it is a present to her
from someone who is among the angels
and is praying for her and for you.

ANNINA, GERMONT, DOCTOR

As long as I have tears to shed,
I shall weep for you.
Soar among the blessed spirits:
God is calling you to him.

ALFREDO

Ah no, death cannot take you
from me so soon.
Ah, live, or a single coffin
shall together enclose us.

VIOLETTA

Show her this picture, *etc.*

(rising up, revived)

How strange!

ANNINA, ALFREDO, GERMONT, DOCTOR
What is it?

VIOLETTA

The spasms of pain
have stopped!
I feel new strength
rising, stirring within me!
Ah, but I'm coming back to life…
What joy!

(She falls back onto the sofa.)

ANNINA, GERMONT, DOTTORE
O cielo!… muor!

ALFREDO
Violetta!…

ANNINA, GERMONT
O Dio, soccorrasi…

DOTTORE *(dopo averle toccata il polso)*
È spenta!

ANNINA, ALFREDO, GERMONT
Oh mio dolor!

(Sipario.)

ANNINA, GERMONT, DOCTOR
Oh Heavens… she's dying!

ALFREDO
Violetta?

ANNINA, GERMONT
O God! Help her!

DOCTOR *(after feeling her pulse)*
She's dead.

ANNINA, ALFREDO, GERMONT
Oh my grief!

(Curtain.)

Select Discography

Recordings have been chosen for their current availability and the interest of their performers. For further performances on disc, see *The Metropolitan Opera Guide to Recorded Opera*, ed. Paul Gruber (London and New York: Thames and Hudson, 1993), pp. 606–17.

YEAR	CAST (VIOLETTA ALFREDO GERMONT)	CONDUCTOR/ORCHESTRA	LABEL
1928*	Mercedes Capsir Lionello Cecil Carlo Galeffi	Lorenzo Molajoli La Scala, Milan	Naxos
1930*	Anna Rosza Alessandro Ziliani Luigi Borgonovi	Carlo Sabajno La Scala, Milan	Opera d'Oro
1946*	Licia Albanese Jan Peerce Robert Merrill	Arturo Toscanini NBC Symphony	RCA Victor
1946*	Adriana Guerrini Luigi Infantino Paolo Silveri	Vincenzo Bellezza Rome Opera	Grammofono 2000
1953*	Maria Callas Francesco Albanese Ugo Savarese	Gabriele Santini Italian Radio Symphony	Warner Classics/ Andromeda
1955	Licia Albanese Giacinto Prandelli Ettore Bastianini	Alberto Erede Metropolitan Opera	Walhall (live)

* mono

1955	Maria Callas Giuseppe di Stefano Ettore Bastianini	Carlo Maria Giulini La Scala, Milan	EMI Classics/ Warner Classics (live)
1955	Antonietta Stella Guiseppe di Stefano Tito Gobbi	Tullio Serafin La Scala, Milan	Naxos
1956	Maria Callas Gianni Raimondi Ettore Bastianini	Carlo Maria Giulini La Scala, Milan	Myto (live)
1956	Rosanna Carteri Cesare Valletti Leonard Warren	Pierre Monteux Rome Opera	RCA/Sony
1958	Maria Callas Alfredo Kraus Mario Sereni	Franco Ghione São Carlos National Theatre, Lisbon	EMI Classics (live)
1958	Maria Callas Cesare Valletti Mario Zanasi	Nicola Rescigno Royal Opera House	ICA Classics (live)
1960	Anna Moffo Richard Tucker Robert Merrill	Fernando Previtali Rome Opera	RCA
1962	Joan Sutherland Carlo Bergonzi Robert Merrill	John Pritchard Maggio Musicale, Florence	Decca
1962	Renata Scotto Gianni Raimondi Ettore Bastianini	Antonino Votto La Scala, Milan	DG
1967	Montserrat Caballé Carlo Bergonzi Sherrill Milnes	Georges Prêtre RCA Italian Opera	RCA Victor

1971	Beverly Sills Nicolai Gedda Rolando Panerai	Aldo Ceccato Royal Philharmonic	EMI Classics/ Warner Classics
1976	Ileana Cotrubas Plácido Domingo Sherrill Milnes	Carlos Kleiber Bayerische Staatsoper	DG
1979	Joan Sutherland Luciano Pavarotti Matteo Manuguerra	Richard Bonynge National Philharmonic	Decca
1980	Renata Scotto Alfredo Kraus Renato Bruson	Riccardo Muti Philharmonia	EMI Classics/ Warner Classics
1981	Valerie Masterson John Brecknock Christian du Plessis	Charles Mackerras ENO	Chandos (in English)
1991	Cheryl Studer Luciano Pavarotti Juan Pons	James Levine Metropolitan Opera	DG
1992	Kiri Te Kanawa Alfredo Kraus Dmitri Hvorostovsky	Zubin Mehta Maggio Musicale, Florence	Philips
1993	Tiziana Fabbricini Roberto Alagna Paolo Coni	Riccardo Muti La Scala, Milan	Sony (live)
1994	Angela Gheorghiu Frank Lopardo Leo Nucci	Georg Solti Royal Opera House	Decca
2005	Anna Netrebko Rolando Villazón Thomas Hampson	Carlo Rizzi Vienna Philharmonic	DG (live)

La traviata on DVD – A Selection

For a fuller listing to 2003, including non-commercial and television films, see Ken Wlaschin, *Encyclopedia of Opera on Screen* (New Haven and London: Yale University Press, 2004), pp. 707–10.

YEAR	CAST (VIOLETTA ALFREDO GERMONT)	CONDUCTOR	DIRECTOR/COMPANY
1967	Anna Moffo Franco Bonisolli Gino Bechi	Giuseppe Patanè Rome Opera House	Mario Lanfranchi Rome Opera House Video Artists Int. (feature film)
1983	Teresa Stratas Plácido Domingo, Cornell MacNeil	James Levine Metropolitan Opera	Franco Zeffirelli Metropolitan Opera DG (feature film)
1988	Marie McLaughlin Walter MacNeil Brent Ellis	Bernard Haitink London Philharmonic	Peter Hall Glyndebourne Festival Arthaus
1992	Edita Gruberová Neil Shicoff Giorgio Zancanaro	Carlo Rizzi Teatro La Fenice	Pier Luigi Pizzi Teatro La Fenice Teldec
1993	Tiziana Fabbricini Roberto Alagna Paolo Coni	Riccardo Muti La Scala	Lilliana Cavani La Scala Sony
1994	Angela Gheorghiu Frank Lopardo Leo Nucci	Georg Solti Royal Opera House	Richard Eyre Royal Opera House Decca

2003	Mireille Delunsch Matthew Polenzani Željko Lučić	Yutaka Sado Orchestre de Paris	Peter Mussbach Festival d'Aix-en- Provence Bel Air
2004	Patrizia Ciofi Roberto Saccà Dmitri Hvorostovsky	Lorin Maazel Teatro La Fenice	Robert Carsen Teatro La Fenice TDK
2005	Anna Netrebko Rolando Villazón Thomas Hampson	Carlo Rizzi Vienna Philharmonic	Willy Decker Salzburg Festival DG
2007	Svetla Vassileva Massimo Giordano Vladimir Stoyano	Yuri Temirkanov Teatro Regio di Parma	Karl-Ernst. & Ursel Hermann Teatro Regio di Parma C Major
2008	Renée Fleming Rolando Villazon Renato Bruson	James Conlon Los Angeles Opera	Marta Domingo Los Angeles Opera Decca
2009	Renée Fleming Joseph Calleja Thomas Hampson	Antonio Pappano Royal Opera House	Richard Eyre Royal Opera House Opus Arte
2011	Natalie Dessay Charles Castronovo Ludovic Tézier	Louis Langrée LSO	Jean-François Sivadier Festival d'Aix-en- Provence Virgin Classics
2011	Marlis Petersen Giuseppe Varano James Rutherford	Tecwyn Evans Graz Philharmonic	Peter Konwitschny Graz Opera Arthaus

Select Bibliography

Abbate, Carolyn and Parker, Roger (eds.), *Analysing Opera: Verdi and Wagner* (Berkeley and Los Angeles: University of California Press, 1989)

Balthazar, Scott L., *The Cambridge Companion to Verdi* (Cambridge: Cambridge University Press, 2004)

Budden, Julian, *The Operas of Verdi*, 3 vols. (London: Cassell, 1973–81, rev. edn., 1992)

Budden, Julian, *Verdi* (Master Musicians Series), (New York: Oxford University Press, 3rd edn, 2008)

Chusid, Martin (ed.), *Verdi's Middle Period, 1849–59: Source Studies, Analysis and Performance Practice* (Chicago: University of Chicago Press, 1997)

Clément, Catherine, trans. Betsy Wing, *Opera, or the Undoing of Women* (London: Virago Press, 1989)

Conati, Marcello (ed.), trans. Richard Stokes, *Interviews and Encounters with Verdi* (London: Gollancz, 1984)

Dumas, Alexandre, trans. Liesl Schillinger, *The Lady of the Camellias* (London: Penguin Books, 2013)

John, Nicholas (ed.), *Violetta and Her Sisters* (London: Faber and Faber, 1994)

Latham, Alison and Parker, Roger (eds.), *Verdi in Performance* (Oxford: Oxford University Press, 2001)

Marvin, Roberta Montemorra, *The Cambridge Verdi Encyclopedia* (Cambridge: Cambridge University Press, forthcoming)

Osborne, Charles, *Letters of Giuseppe Verdi* (London: Gollancz, 1971)

Parker, Roger, *The New Grove Guide to Verdi and his Operas* (New York: Oxford University Press, 2009)

Phillips-Matz, Mary Jane, *Verdi, A Biography* (Oxford: Oxford University Press, 1993)

Rosselli, John, *The Life of Verdi* (Cambridge: Cambridge University Press, 2000)

Weaver, William, *Verdi: A Documentary Study* (London: Thames and Hudson, 1977)

Weaver, William and Chusid, Martin (eds.), *The Verdi Companion* (New York: Norton, 1979)

Verdi Websites*

In English or with an English-language option

Verdi 200   www.giuseppeverdi.it/visInglese

List of stage works   opera.stanfor.edu/Verdi/main.html

Complete La traviata *discography*
                    operadis-opera-discography.org.uk/CLVETRAV.HTM

* Links valid at the time of publication in 2013.

Note on the Contributors

Denis Arnold was Professor of Music at the University of Nottingham and Heather Professor of Music at Oxford University. He was editor of *The New Oxford Companion to Music*. He also broadcast frequently and wrote regularly for *Gramophone*.

Nicholas John was ENO's Literary Editor and Dramaturg. He was series editor of the original John Calder opera guides and editor of *Power House: The English National Opera Experience* and *Violetta and Her Sisters*.

Roger Parker is Thurston Dart Professor of Music at King's College London. He is General Editor (with Gabriele Dotto) of the Donizetti critical edition. His most recent book is *A History of Opera: The Last Four Hundred Years*, written jointly with Carolyn Abbate.

Anna Picard trained as a singer at the Royal Academy of Music before working in the field of Early Music. From 2000 to 2013, she was Classical Music Critic for the *Independent on Sunday*. She also contributes to *Opera* and *BBC Music Magazine*.

Hugo Shirley is a classical music and opera critic for the *Daily Telegraph*, Deputy Editor of *Opera* and an Early Career Research Fellow at Oxford Brookes University.

Acknowledgements

We would like to thank John Allison of *Opera*, John Pennino of the Metropolitan Opera, Charles Johnston and Mike Ashman for their assistance and advice in the preparation of this guide.

www.overturepublishing.com
www.eno.org